MW00782356

INTERIOR SPLENDOR
BY PIERRE-YVES ROCHON

DANE McDOWELL
PHOTOGRAPHS BY CHRISTIAN SARRAMON

Flammarion

CONTENTS

FACING PAGE
Butterflies and birds of paradise
lend refinement to the blue silk
of an armchair.

FOLLOWING PAGES
The renovations in the lobby
of the Hôtel des Bergues reveal
once again its magnificent
neoclassical proportions.

FOREWORD

The word "luxury" evokes strong reactions, not all of them positive. For some it suggests superfluity, a kind of sumptuous expenditure in a quest for ostentation. Such excessive refinement can be perceived as elitist, shallow, or, at its most extreme, immoral.

Yet this is the very opposite of the concept so wonderfully developed by Pierre-Yves Rochon. For Rochon, a true sense of luxury—which is what he creates—is neither aggressive nor showy. In fact, he argues that this sense of luxury exists deep inside every one of us, although it may never surface. Most people have it without realizing it.

Luxury is the child of a desire for abundance, and as such it should be recognized that nature, rather than firmly rejecting luxury, positively encourages it. Nature is fundamentally luxuriant: heady flowers, lush fruit, cascading waters, crackling fires, frothy seas, magnificently tinted sunsets.

Luxury means transcending the ordinary, the everyday. Living elsewhere.

Luxury means enjoying rewards; exorcising the dreariness of everyday life; fulfilling normal desires; satisfying fantasies of experiencing and having everything. It means attaining the exceptional.

It is difficult to overcome the temptation to go overboard, which happens easily enough. Luxury calls for discretion and harmony, for a mental alchemy that is not always easy to master.

Rochon is one of the few interior designers who has attained such mastery, as demonstrated by his success. He is at home in every realm—hotels, private apartments, restaurants, office spaces—and on every continent, from Europe and the Americas to the Middle East and Far East.

A designer's creative talent begins in childhood and evolves through successive metamorphoses, like a fundamental process of nature: the bud gives way to the flower, which is replaced by the fruit that itself perishes in the victorious new plant. For Rochon, two concretely influential phases seem to be particularly important when it comes to grasping his originality. The first is an accident of birth: as the son of a military officer, from the very beginning Rochon experienced the discipline that would structure his personality. Being a stickler for detail is important when it comes to achieving excellence. Furthermore, Rochon's birthright opened his eyes to the world: even as a child he knew that things happened "elsewhere." As his family moved from barracks to barracks—North Africa, the Middle East—the young Rochon was exposed to Islamic art and civilization, so different from his family's European traditions. It is interesting to imagine the impressions left on the mind of a child (and, later, sensitive young man) by this openness, this escape from the closed environment of France. The idea of impressions, the very word, relates to the second important influence on Rochon.

No creative artist conceives and executes a work in an isolated state of innate talent. Creation is also re-creation, because it calls for multiple inputs.

Enter Lucchino Visconti, whose films were a revelation to Rochon. However, the riot of velvets and silks, the exuberance of gold and marble, the harmony of the drapery, the boldness of the framing are far from explaining his full influence. Rochon would also find in Visconti a justification of—and spur to—his desire for luxury.

So did Rochon imitate Visconti?

No, of course not. Nor did Visconti slavishly reproduce the existing palaces that he used for film sets. Instead, he modified them according to his mood, his fantasies, the needs of his genius. Visconti, too, was an artist who re-created.

The brevity of this foreword inevitably means excluding many of Rochon's other sources of inspiration, such as his love of travel, which has spurred so many discoveries; his passion for the graphic arts; or an intense curiosity that leads him to scour museums and constantly seek new encounters.

Should we end here? Well, yes, of course. Because more important than any analysis is the act of opening this book. It is in Rochon's work that readers will discover what luxury brings—a true, if perhaps unacknowledged, degree of happiness.

FRANÇOIS GALL

FACING PAGE In Florence, luxury always seeks to be authentic. A green silk bedspread harmonizes wonderfully
with the magnificent hand-painted wall panel, based on artwork of the period and created by an artisan from London.
FOLLOWING PAGE A grand hotel in Florence has turned a private chapel into a tearoom where Directoire-style furnishings
and Renaissance frescoes make for an unforgettable moment of peace and quiet.

INTRODUCTION

Pierre-Yves Rochon, Interior Designer

Have you ever noticed how, after unpacking your bags in a hotel room after a long and tiring journey, a delightful feeling of well-being suddenly sweeps over you? Like magic, travel fatigue melts away. Jet-lag vanishes. All that remains is the pleasure of relaxing in a plush environment where luxury is present in countless little ways, where colors are orchestrated around a special palette, where comfort can be savored in a soft bed or a carefully lit bathroom. Interior decoration has reconciled you to the world—and to yourself. It creates a setting that is far from neutral or innocent.

The details that bring such pleasure have nothing to do with the quality of service in a grand hotel. They are the product of lengthy thought about what makes an environment harmonious. Who has managed to create this enveloping feeling of sweet comfort and privacy, expressed with so much subtlety and refinement? Within the competitive profession of interior design one name comes to mind—and not just on both sides of the Atlantic, but as far as the shores of the China Sea. The same name has come to mind for the past thirty years: Pierre-Yves Rochon.

Hanging in the hall of a hotel in Paris, a small picture discreetly sums up Rochon's philosophy. It is not a portrait or a landscape, but a saying from Georges Braque, which sounds as though it came from the mouth of an interior designer: *J'aime la règle qui corrige l'émotion* ("I like rules that discipline emotion"). In half a dozen words, it says it all: after a first impression that provokes an emotional response, the eye lingers on the surroundings, analyzing each component and appreciating the results of exquisite discipline. In all the work that bears Rochon's signature, each element has been chosen according to a personal logic that combines function, space, convenience, and appearance. The interior is distinguished by its elegance, not by extravagance, and is based on a discreet symbolism that shuns the ostentatious.

It is impossible to speak of a specific style, because no two interiors are alike and because Rochon never falls prey to passing fashions and trends. He can shift brilliantly from neoclassicism to minimalism; he loves both marquetry furniture and modern design. "Creativity knows no period or borders," says the designer in all earnestness. "I like mixing styles, adding touches of modernity to a classic image. I create unifying combinations."

This eclecticism is typical of Rochon's work, setting him apart from other interior designers. Yet with sincere modesty he never mentions the reasons for his fame; he prefers to discuss the main lines of his craft, a profession in which imagination, knowledge, and observation are closely linked. The role of an interior designer, he says, is to create public and private spaces by devising pleasing environments that meet a client's wishes. After studying the client's guidelines, Rochon draws up plans and sketches to depict the proposed transformation. Thanks to

J'aime la
règle
qui corrige
l'émotion.

G Braque

Page 1 sur 1

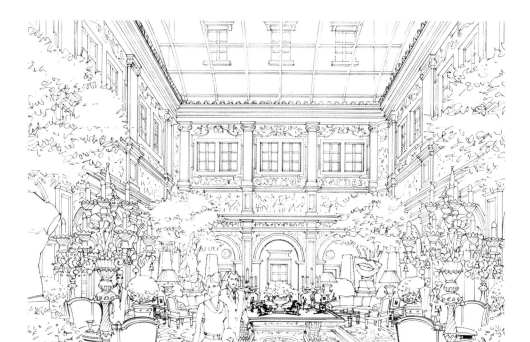

computer technology, such plans are now astonishingly precise. Then, having obtained the client's approval, the interior designer contacts various contractors and draws up a schedule to insure the progress and monitoring of the project. It is the designer, as main contractor, who coordinates the whole construction site via his own team. He must combine a talent for observation with artistic intuition and common sense, and must furthermore keep abreast of new technology and the latest trends in design. Taking radically different roles into account, the designer brings them all together, a synthesis of elements that cohere in the overall project. Every new project is a creative act, one that corresponds to an artistic vision of a contemporary lifestyle that is able, simultaneously, to acknowledge the past.

But if all these projects are the work of the same designer, why do they all look so individual, so unlike one another? Rochon pauses, smiles, and then somewhat indirectly delivers the secret of his professional success. "I hate the uniformity of grand international hotels, where every room is identical and grimly impersonal. I am first of all an architectural designer, and then a decorator, and I envisage every hotel as a second home, 'a home away from home.'" It is therefore hardly surprising that his interiors do not resemble one another.

Rochon won't talk about all the compliments he receives for his work. You have to learn about them from other people. The American press, usually so stinting of praise when it comes to French designers, showers kudos on Rochon. And Britain's *Financial Times,* in an article on the "masters of *grande luxe*," paid tribute to his constant inventiveness, his opulently elegant style, and his absolute mastery of details. The *FT* pointed out that for the designers of Europe's grandest hotels, "it's not enough to be great—they need to be the best."

Meanwhile, the Michelin-starred chef Alain Ducasse, with whom Rochon has collaborated on projects in France and abroad, stresses one single point: "Every interior designed by Pierre-Yves Rochon is just right."

Who is the man behind this great designer? A visit to his office on Avenue Matignon in Paris reveals a glimpse of the master at work. Imagine two entire floors designed to be functional, sober, and strikingly elegant. At first glance, it looks like a private home. There is a calm, masculine atmosphere: on a dark gray carpet, the furniture is a combination of dark wood, leather, and chrome. On the walls these same, somewhat cool, tones dominate the abstract paintings. And although it is not a frivolous place, behind the doors a closely knit team exudes talent and dynamism. One vast room lined with shelves from floor to ceiling contains hundreds of samples of textiles and other materials such as parquet flooring, marbles, and mosaics.

PAGE 10
Pierre-Yves Rochon at work, pencil always in hand.

PAGE 11
Françoise Durst's samples of fabrics and mounting boards lead to the perfect framing of a Romantic portrait.

FACING PAGE
The entrance hall to an art deco house by the sea.

ABOVE
A freehand drawing of the marble courtyard at the Four Seasons in Florence.

PAGE 14
Elegantly modern chairs designed by Rochon.

PAGE 15
At the Sofitel Chicago Water Tower, Rochon devised a spectacular opalescent wall that serves as a setting for the monumental staircase of black glass.

Next door, members of his team are entering an impressive number of designs, plans, and eleva-
tions into their computers. Another room looks like a conference area, while yet another is packed
with furniture and accessories. Further away, at the end of a hall dotted with original drawings
and engravings, is the quiet, spacious office of Rochon himself. This is where, for the first time in
his career, he has agreed to talk about himself and his secret art of creating just the right interior.

"As far back as I can remember," he says, "I've always been moved by beauty. It's a real
feeling that lights up my life, both professionally and personally." Ever since he was a young
boy Rochon has drawn, painted, and observed, and so it was not surprising that he enrolled in
a college of fine arts, where he graduated first in his class.

"I was like a sponge. I absorbed everything they taught me. But above all, I liked the
restraint and elegance. And I still do nowadays! I was the only student to wear a jacket and tie."

He harbored a secret dream of becoming a movie director. "I loved American comedies
of the 1940s and '50s, preferably in black and white, and I would go crazy over the visual
perfection of movie sets in those days. The oversized majesty of volumes, the vast bay windows and French doors draped with magnificent curtains, the beauty of all that furniture
with sober lines."

Already drawn to the spectacle of luxury, whether expressed with rigor or flaunted with
impertinence, Rochon became captivated by the historical reconstructions and flamboyant
direction of the films of Luchino Visconti. It was not the opulence but rather the sensitivity,
the lyricism, the sense of detail, the artistic effect, and the intelligent staging that enchanted
Rochon.

His own professional career, however, began with a pencil rather than a camera in hand.
On graduating from art school, he worked for Michel Boyer for ten years. He then founded
his own agency. Once on his own, there was no margin for error—but difficulties, far from
worrying Rochon, stimulate him. "What I like about such varied projects is the constantly
renewed challenge. The only way to do things is to demand total competence," he points out.

PAGE 16
The Royal Suite in the
Four Seasons Hotel in Florence
undergoing restoration.

PAGE 17
A drawing of the curtains
for the new ballroom.

FACING PAGE AND ABOVE
Tableware puts the finishing touch
to an interior. The pattern of the
china used in the Grand-Hôtel du
Cap-Ferrat was designed freehand
by Rochon after a painting
by Matisse, while his rose-and-
ribbon pattern for a china service
at the Hôtel George V in Paris
was inspired by a rose garden.

LEFT
A lounge in Monte Carlo
Bay creates a nautical
atmosphere in which
a porthole-shaped mirror
reflects the image
of a sailboat.

"Taking risks, refusing to base my work on a signature style, seeking variety by totally invent-ing a contemporary setting or interpreting a historic one in my own way is more than just a challenge—it's a pleasure."

Curious by nature, Rochon is a great traveler. He learns something in every country he visits. Through simple application of common sense, he has arrived at the same results espoused in Eastern approaches to interiors—namely, that every element in an interior should be designed to please the eye, the mind, and the body. He has also learned that beauty and function go together, that aesthetics and ethics are closely related. Thus the rational arrangement of stor-age space and the use of high-quality materials for utilitarian items—from faucets to spare furnishings—enhance everyday life. Through calligraphy, Rochon has explored the dialogue between upstrokes and downstrokes, between solids and voids, and has learned to empty space in order to valorize a given feature or item of furniture. "Like the Japanese, I think beauty lies in simplicity," he says. "The simpler the interior, the more quality will stand out; the smaller the space, the more you must pay scrupulous attention to details."

Although Rochon travels a good deal and spends a certain amount of time in his Chicago office, he still feels fundamentally European. In addition to his favorite country, France, he loves Italy, where beauty is still an inextricable part of daily life, something that is obvious to all the senses, and has nothing to do with the dictatorship of technology. "We should never forget," continues Rochon, "that our work is addressed to all five senses, and therefore involves a well-orchestrated sensuality. Which still has to be adapted to each case! Since I've spent much of my career restructuring grand hotels, I've acquired a certain experience. And yet I still have to explain to hotel managers the many ways of preparing for the arrival of clients so that guests feel right at home. What is the best way to welcome a person or a couple in a place that is unfa-miliar to them? By playing the role of a 'total stranger' who enters a hotel room for the first

ABOVE
Rochon designed a carpet
in an art deco spirit based
on harmonies of red and gold.

FACING PAGE
"Just the right luxuriousness"
for a bed: a symphony of red—
pillowcases with flat edgings,
and cushions covered in silk.
Note the finish on the bedspread
with its coordinated piping.

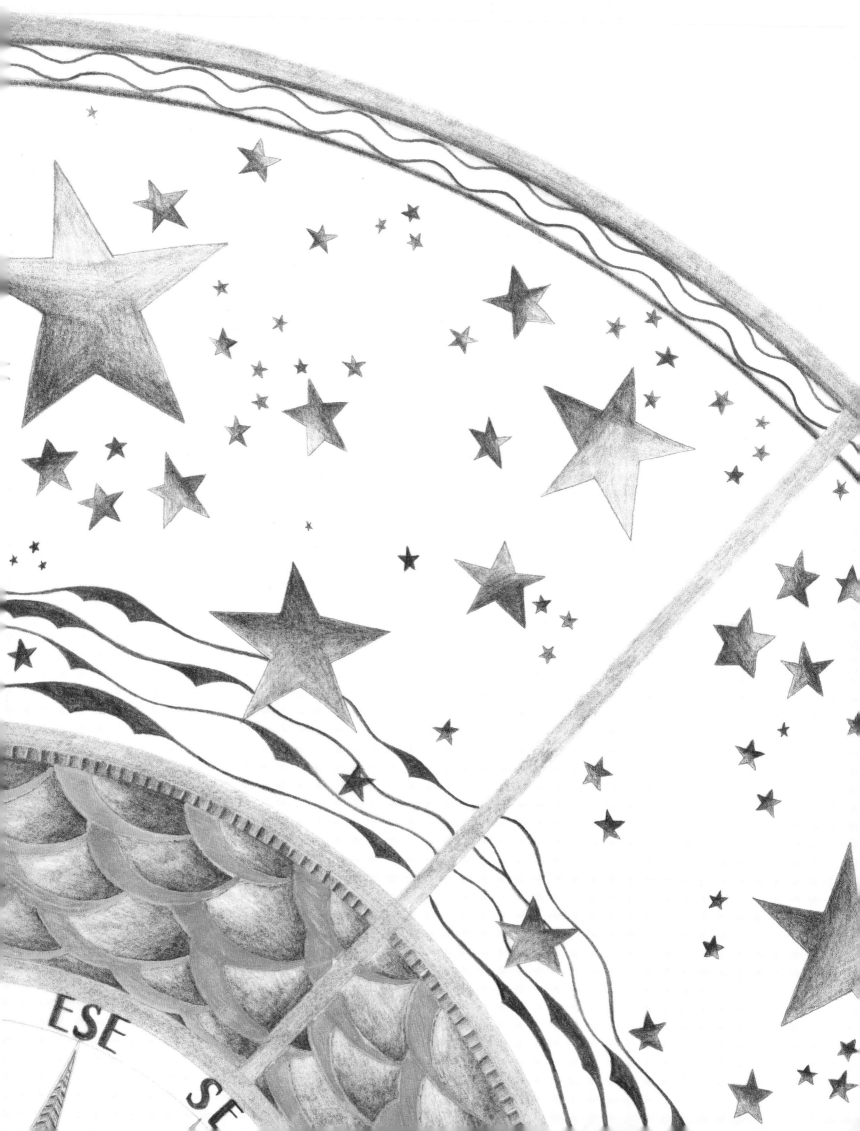

time, you can figure out how to personalize an interior, to give it some much-needed touches of warmth, to add the detail that changes everything. I make sure it's perfect, I check everything, from flattering lighting in the bathroom, to details in the bedroom that lead the eye toward the essential thing: harmonious volumes and colors, the immaculate whiteness of bed linen, the double row of pillows on the large-sized bed, a tastefully framed picture on the wall. I examine not only the silken texture and drape of curtains, but also their lining, which must provide a soothing darkness."

The principles applied to luxury hotels are the same for a private home or apartment. Is the judicious combination of subjective and objective, of rational and emotional, of instinct and intellect, enough to explain the secret of a successful interior? The designer pauses before commenting, "The spirit of the place is still my main source of inspiration. There is always a story to be told, which I use to establish my primary themes."

It's no secret that what truly drives this extreme perfectionist to challenge himself constantly and overcome constraints are his passionate energy and his love of work well done. You only do well what you love.

"You can't create if you're not a dreamer," asserts Rochon. And, with a smile, he recounts a true story: once, while he was explaining the importance of dreams to his own work, a potential client interrupted him by saying, "I'm not paying anybody to dream!" Obviously, this comment put an end to any future collaboration.

For Rochon, reverie is a source of inventiveness. More than just an aid to staging, it is a liberating experience that blurs obstacles the better to bring feelings into sharp focus. Rochon owes his bold moves, his extravagant combinations of colors, his impertinent anachronisms, and his crazy ideas to reverie and dream. To keep "in practice," Rochon designs fantasy settings

PAGE 24
At the Ritz Carlton
in Bahrain, Rochon drew
on astral and oceanic motifs
when designing a glass dome that
crowns the 32-foot-high atrium.

PAGE 25
A detail of the design.

FACING PAGE
A lobby with its black marble floor
prompts passersby to pause
to admire the marble column
along which elevators rise.

ABOVE
A detail of the blue and beige
carpet specially designed
for the hotel in a 1930s spirit.

Incorporating a bathroom
and dressing room into a hotel
that is a historic landmark
is no easy task. Rochon designed
a partition separating the bed
and the bathroom, allowing
a wonderful view of the painted
ceiling from the bathtub.

FACING PAGE
Sometimes the flooring sets
the tone for an interior.
Rochon designed this marble
inlay that graces the floor
of the Hôtel George V in Paris.

FOLLOWING PAGES
In Rochon's office on Avenue
Matignon in Paris, order,
quiet, and concentration reign.

such as an interior for Maison & Objet: a lavish white living room whose snowy softness was the delight of polar bears, creating a fairy-tale world in which every visitor briefly became a child again. Rochon's "Orientalist" interiors, meanwhile, are like waking dreams, a delightful netherworld with a whiff of the forbidden. When it comes to his versions of eighteenth-century design, they seem like motionless journeys through a world of grace, balance, and beauty

For the first time, Rochon has agreed to publish his work. At the height of his career, this man in a hurry—always on his way to another airport—has decided to share his skills and his approach to beauty. By inviting readers to view the exclusive premises that bear his signature, Rochon is encouraging them to draw inspiration from this teeming kaleidoscope of harmonies and atmospheres; he is spurring them to soak up ideas and advice in order to re-invent, in their own ways, a finer lifestyle, a realm full of refinement and joy.

CHAPTER I

Stagecraft

> " I think of the work of an interior designer as I would a theater production. I imagine the scenario, the setting, and the lighting. "

Certain places, like certain encounters, are impossible to forget. But it isn't lavishness—or a slavish obedience to passing fashion—that generates the persistence of memory. It is the emotion experienced at a specific time that triggers our ability to recall, which is what Pierre-Yves Rochon seeks when beginning a new project.

"Fine volumes and space are my idea of luxury," he stresses. Working in the United States is a real pleasure because space is readily available, a boon which has allowed Rochon to pursue original ideas without restraint, as seen at the Sofitel Chicago Water Tower.

In Europe, everything has to begin with the restructuring of space. A harmonious relationship of volumes creates a dynamic in which each element resonates with the others. Without violating the spirit of a place, Rochon creates openings, knocks down partition walls, and brings two rooms together to obtain a liberating expanse of space. He employs light and voids lavishly. Voids are used to expand, refine, and create tension within solids. Light is used to sculpt and transform space. "If used correctly," Rochon explains, "artificial light adds depth and height, re-establishing the balance that is so important to me. I've also been making greater use of mirrors, as I've just done at the Pré Catelan restaurant in Paris. Mirrors can be used to multiply the sense of space by capturing light. I set them in the embrasures of windows to draw the garden indoors—they're wonderful devices!"

Because he likes to compose scenes like a painter, Rochon creates perspectives that lead the eye and help it grasp the essential. For pure visual pleasure he will create long alignments, or break the monotony of a hallway with a rotunda, as at Les Crayères in Reims, France; he monitors the symmetry of volumes, not hesitating to place false doors in the wall of a sitting room if the architectonic balance calls for it.

"When dealing with a renovation project, you have to remember that people systematically lowered ceilings in the 1970s in order to fill the space with pipes and wires. Technology has become my great enemy," he complains, "complicating life and robbing space. But what can you do about it? You have to do everything over, minimizing the loss of space by using more recent techniques to squeeze in essential equipment. Sometimes you can cheat a little. Instead of retaining the full height, you can lower the ceiling of an entrance hall, which magnifies the volume of the adjacent lounge. By creating differences you can correct flaws—it's a simple question of optics!"

Color is the second powerful tool of stagecraft. For this former fine-art student, it is color that defines a setting, establishes an atmosphere. Blue is traditionally associated with peace and tranquility,

PAGE 32
Rochon drew inspiration from the blue of the extraordinary Renaissance painted ceiling when choosing under-curtains and velvet upholstery.

FACING PAGE
This lounge in the Monte-Carlo Bay Hotel has a nautical atmosphere; the huge photo of a sailboat in a regatta is an allegory for modern adventure.

making it ideal for a bedroom. Because he excels in coordinating hues of this emblematic color, Rochon has been nicknamed the Grand Master of Blue. The lounges and rooms in Les Crayères, like the suites at the Hôtel George V in Paris, are settings of extreme refinement, where walls of azure, pale blue, royal and turquoise blue are echoed by coordinated tones of silks, stuccowork, and woodwork.

And yet Rochon acknowledges his love of bright red, a sensual and stimulating color that he deploys in surprisingly bold monochromes. Rarely would a private homeowner think of using such a brilliant hue in this way—it requires daring, says Rochon. Red favors intimacy, as demonstrated by the sensual ambience of the suites in the Grand Hôtel du Lac in Vevey, Switzerland. Red is also a festive, theatrical color used from floor to ceiling in the restaurants he has designed with Joël Robuchon, as well as the dining room of the Hotel Sacher in Vienna. Then there is the cardinal red used along the hallway of Les Crayères, enlivening the entire floor. To add a touch of modernity or exoticism to a lounge or living room, Rochon might underscore red with black. And Rochon sometimes contrasts his red with green, a refreshing color that often figures on his palette. Green reigns supreme in a sublime bedroom in the Sacher, where Rochon creates a subtle blend of splendor and delicate refinement.

"I love harmonies based on either subtle shades or radical contrasts," says Rochon. As an expert in the art of chromatic counterpoint, he can envisage powerful dialogues between opposing hues. He thus transformed the Hôtel Keppler in Paris from a traditional hotel into a contemporary venue by orchestrating black and white. By juxtaposing patterns and textures he can also reappropriate artworks with wit and coherence. "These playful contrasts, which are what I like best, dominate the interior of my own house in Brittany," he admits.

Such scenic effects do not prevent Rochon from dealing with softer tones. At the Four Seasons Hotel in Florence, the opulence of the staging is alternately tempered and intensified through shades of violet and purple. In Paris, the golden brown marble in the entrance of the Hôtel George V inspired Rochon's renovation of the premises in yellows, pale gold, and ivory. At the Paris Ritz, it is a discreet yet elegant gray that adorns the finest suites in the hotel.

So does the impact of an interior depend exclusively on the harmony of volumes and the resonance of colors? No, because other important factors contribute to a sense of total physical and mental comfort, namely the quality of materials and the refinement of execution. These features, a testament to Rochon's sure, demanding taste, are an integral part of his stagecraft. They are discussed in the next chapter.

FACING PAGE
The spectacular lobby of a grand hotel in Monaco impresses guests with its marble flooring, giant vases, and glass archway, all enhanced by subtle lighting.

ABOVE
The harmony of the veined marble of the walls and floor in this Viennese interior is illuminated by gilt-bronze wall lamps.

IN FLORENCE

A unique way to enjoy the Renaissance
wonders of Florence entails a stay
in the Four Seasons Hotel renovated
by Rochon. The designer instilled new life
into a fifteenth-century palazzo
and a sixteenth-century convent through
an imposing interior that is the height
of luxury and comfort, all the while
respecting the spirit of the original periods.
Walls and woodwork flaunt the colors
of Tuscany beneath the frescoes
and bas-reliefs dotted with gilded
stuccowork, trompe-l'œil, and silks.

PRECEDING PAGES Draped in violet-colored silk that harmonizes with the color palette of the ceiling, a bed *à la polonaise* beckons the weary traveler. The stylized foliage of the bedspread and bench echo the baroque swirls of the gilded wood bedstead. FACING PAGE Below the extraordinary painted ceilings in the gallery on the *piano nobile*, modern sofas cohabit with period furniture. Dating from the fifteenth century, the original painted floor tiles hold their own against costly Oriental carpets. In the background, an allegorical sculpture in stucco crowns the doorway. ABOVE The door of the main entrance, a sober variant on the arches of the gallery on the *piano nobile*, opens onto a romantic garden.

ABOVE In the hotel spa, an unusual Chinese-inspired stand serves as a showcase for alabaster and porcelain objects. The antique-style decor includes cushions adorned with Greek profiles beneath a *grisaille* painting. FACING PAGE In this room the *pietra serena* style of the columns and the gray Tuscan stone harmonizes with the white Carrara marble on the floor. The clean lines of a modern sofa sit well with the Directoire-style ornamentation. FOLLOWING PAGES Even if the lace-collared gentleman invited her in, the Venus of the Bath would never venture into the blue sitting room *di Conventino*. The brocade damask upholstery of the Louis XVI armchairs and sofa complement the checkerboard marble flooring.

ABOVE The jade-colored bedspread, punctuated by silk and velvet cushions, responds subtly to the damask and velvet curtains that open onto the garden. FACING PAGE What wonderful dreams must be dreamed beneath this extraordinary painted ceiling in the Royal Suite, featuring a pope flanked by cherubs! Rochon emphasized the importance of treasures from the past by incorporating Chinese hand-painted silk panels depicting birds among blossoms.

FACING PAGE AND ABOVE In this same suite, the furnishings made by local Florentine artisans are an integral part of a lavish setting in which every detail—parquet floor, precious carpets, objets d'art, Louis XVI armchairs, fabrics of silk, velvet, and damask—contributes to the sumptuous whole.

PRECEDING PAGES The Florentine *dolce vita* evolves with the changing hour—here, golden light barely caresses the painted frescoes on the ceiling. Each object has been chosen to echo a costly fabric or a period painting. ABOVE AND FACING PAGE To appreciate the extraordinary work entailed in restoring the palazzo, you must pause at every step, and survey your surroundings from floor to ceiling. As a pendant to the mythological scenes, Rochon designed the mosaic flooring from four colored marbles: the dark gray of Bleu de Savoie, the lighter gray of *pietra serena*, the red of Verona, and the white of Carrara. The staging of the palazzo and former convent is a paean to authenticity and accuracy, making this one of the most beautiful hotels in the world.

II

IN MONACO,
BETWEEN SEA
AND GARDEN

Opened just a few years ago,
the Monte-Carlo Bay
Hotel and Resort, creates a true holiday
atmosphere in the principality of Monaco.
Commissioned to execute the interior
design, Rochon chose a palette
of Mediterranean hues for the rooms
and spacious suites that overlook
the sea and a luxuriant, exotic garden.
Enjoying spectacular space
and a contemporary atmosphere,
the lounges, bars, and restaurants
are relaxed, chic meeting places
for gilded—and moneyed—youth.

PRECEDING PAGES Impressive vases and an oversized basin welcome the guests of the spa. Soft lighting is an invitation to a health cure or beauty session. FACING PAGE Paved with black marble and punctuated by tall red columns, the main hall is accentuated by the generosity of its dimensions. ABOVE In a lounge with a masculine feel, suitable for discussing business or swapping secrets, a pair of coral vases catches the eye. A specially designed piece of furniture adorns the way to the *Grande Galerie* overlooking the exotic gardens, which ensures the privacy of the guests by a clever use of space.

ABOVE Lighting plays a key role in interiors. Designed by Stéphane Rochon, a vertical panel changes color to dazzle visitors night and day. Heavenly blue extends into the hotel bar with its starry ceiling. FACING PAGE Opposite the reception desk, a small lounge is a comfortable spot to await latecomers or prepare for an important meeting.

PRECEDING PAGES The landing has a surprisingly dramatic effect: highlighted by a blue light, the spiral shape of the bold central sofa is made the center of attraction. The aquatic and floral themes of the abstract paintings are a reminder of the hotel's location on the Mediterranean coast. FACING PAGE In the suite with coral-red walls, Rochon favored a contemporary ambience with clean-lined furnishings and sober touches of black wood. The office follows this same color scheme—with a dark desk placed on a vermilion rug with geometric patterns. ABOVE Every detail—in the bedroom, sitting room, and bathroom—displays the same discipline and harmony.

III

VIENNA WITH
AN OPERATIC AIR

The Hotel Sacher, located between
St Stephen's Cathedral and the Vienna
State Opera, is a landmark
in the Austrian capital. Rochon
revisited this legendary venue,
devising a magnificent setting inspired
by the glorious years of the Hapsburg
dynasty. Rediscovering the original
spirit created by Franz Sacher in 1872,
and simultaneously providing
a fine setting for a splendid collection
of nineteenth-century paintings,
Rochon has produced a collection
of refined, lavish atmospheres designed
to thrill lovers of opera
and neoclassical architecture.

PRECEDING PAGES Time has come to a halt in the large red lounge. The dark woodwork provides a precious setting for this sumptuous yet intimate room. The brocade-upholstered armchairs and sofas beneath the large chandelier await music-lovers for a chat over a cup of tea. ABOVE Pleated silk lampshades screen the light cast on the little glossy black tables and the carpet with stylized foliate motif. FACING PAGE The hotel entrance, lined in velvet and red brocade, is lit like an opera set, creating a marvelous realm that is a tribute to the opera stars and other celebrities who have frequented the hotel for more than a century.

PRECEDING PAGES Jade green is the refreshing yet refined color chosen by Rochon for this suite with neoclassical decoration. A red bench and armchairs brighten the tone. The indefinable luxury of this room arises from the alchemy of the canopied bed, the crystal chandelier, the embroidered cushions, and lavish silken fabrics. FACING PAGE AND ABOVE A twentieth-century Viennese bed of carved wood reigns in one luxurious suite. The green velvet sofa and bench are matched by the silk cushions on the bed and wall coverings. At the head of the bed, a period painting adds a refined, individual note to this little setting, giving the visitor the delightful impression of being the guest of a noble Viennese family.

ABOVE The marble bathrooms hark back to majestic Roman baths but a contemporary interior also finds its way into the legendary Hotel Sacher. In one, a blue light plays on the marble; in another, a game of mirrors separates the bedroom from the bathroom. FACING PAGE An eighteenth-century console table and a bouquet of roses complete the decor of a landing that sports bold yet elegant stripes under the classical molding of the ceiling.

FACING PAGE Rochon dared to combine toile de Jouy and striped fabrics in a harmony of pale blues—one of his favorite, and wonderfully successful, exercises in style. ABOVE Every detail, from the wall lamps to the bedstead to the choice of artworks, obeys a rigor that nevertheless admits bold moves. The radically modern bathroom features appealingly pure geometry.

PRECEDING PAGES "You shouldn't be afraid of color." This belief of Pierre-Yves Rochon is expressed in the Hotel Sacher through a palette of "imperial" colors of blue and gold. The blue brocade is highlighted by the gold of the bar, which is also picked up in the Belle Époque portraits. FACING PAGE AND ABOVE Red and green damask and textured velvets cover the walls and padded furniture, creating a lavish *fin de siècle* atmosphere.

IV

PLACE VENDÔME

The name alone of the legendary
Ritz hotel evokes the high point
of Parisian living. The luxury hotel
was built in 1705 and then
transformed at the end of the nineteenth century for César Ritz.
Rochon has recently restored
several suites to chic elegance,
introducing elements of modernity
into the neoclassical decor so that
the traveler can savor the refined
atmosphere in complete comfort.
A slight transformation of spaces,
and a choice of soft colors enhanced
by black and gold, introduce
a twenty-first century spirit
to an eighteenth-century style,
and will no doubt attract
new generations of writers.

PRECEDING PAGES A delicate spectrum of grays underlined with gold shows the classical beauty of the suite. The transformed space is set off by the moldings and the specially designed friezes, and is filtered by the sumptuous gray silk curtains. Drawing on the famous hotel's own heritage, Rochon selected period furniture and magnificent bronzes that stand out against the delicate woodwork. A feminine note is added through scattered touches of pink—here on an armchair or there on a velvet cushion, or again on the pleated silk of a lampshade.
FACING PAGE AND ABOVE The gilding on the frames, bedstead, and edging on the lacquered black table come to life against the pearl-gray damask walls. Rochon rearranged the distribution of space to create a real entranceway and dressing room. Based on harmonies of gray, pink, and black, this interior reflects a savoir faire that draws on modern technology as well as eighteenth-century refinement.

ABOVE Whereas black adorns the washroom in the entrance, white and gold create a neoclassical atmosphere in the bathroom. Every detail of the suite illustrates the refinement of the design: the combination of black and gold, the detail on the lampshades, the mirror, and the crystal birds. FACING PAGE A large eighteenth-century painting with a gilded wood frame adds a refined, poetic touch to the suite. The legs of the bronze table harmonize with the fine-gold patina of the armchairs *à la reine*.

IV

IN VEVEY

The Grand Hôtel du Lac opened
in 1868 and has aged with grace,
but Pierre-Yves Rochon recently
injected some new blood into it
by redesigning everything. He created
a coherent interior that is
as comfortable as possible yet has that
"something extra." As Rochon said,
"I didn't want to create a hotel,
I wanted a home—elegant
and private." The result is one
of his finest accomplishments.

PRECEDING PAGES The small Eastern-influenced lounge is like the embodiment of one of Thomas de Quincey's opium dreams. The wrought-iron metalwork acts like a threshold between dreams and reality. A commode and Syrian pedestal tables spur reveries of travel under the pensive gaze of a sultana with a fan. FACING PAGE AND ABOVE The dream-like quality is conveyed by an extravagant profusion of silks and brocades, by harmonies of gold and sea-blue velvet, and by tasseled curtains and crystal wall lamps from Turkey.

PRECEDING PAGES An entirely red room is a daring accomplishment. Only slightly offset by a beige-striped wall, the red of the curtains, bed, and cushions accentuates the theatrical aspect of the room by being reflected in the mirrored bedside tables. FACING PAGE In this boudoir decorated with toile de Jouy fabric, a skillful play of reflections in the mirror and Italian commode catches the daylight. ABOVE In the lounge of the suite, gold is also picked out on the Louis XVI chairs, the sofa, the curtains, and the walls of the entrance. A ravishing Indian console and crystal wall-lights add to the luxurious feel.

ABOVE AND FACING PAGE In the lounge overlooking the lake, Rochon created a symphony of blue and gray underscored by dark-wood furniture. On the sofa, silk cushions pick up the chrysanthemum theme on the Chinese screen. The filtered light creates a soft, peaceful atmosphere, as befits a stay by the lake. The original mosaic that leads to the lounge has been restored to its former state.

CHAPTER II

In Search of Total Comfort

> " I wanted to create hotels that were like homes, my objective being to create an atmosphere which was at once refined and comfortable... a celebration of elegance and good taste. "

The remembrance of writers past still lingers in the deserted hallways of grand hotels early in the morning. What did such writers seek here, if not a somewhat rarefied universe? At the Ritz in Paris, Marcel Proust would venture out wrapped in a shawl, and would dine alone in a private salon, in quest of luxury, peace, and harmony. Nowadays, this feeling of well-being and elegance can be had by passing through the revolving doors of any of the premises transformed by Pierre-Yves Rochon. Guests enter an enchanted world where the lavish setting and plush ambience abolish time and dreariness. Every element adds to the magic of the place: marble, gilded stucco, sumptuous floral arrangements, crystal chandeliers with glittering reflections, silken brocade on the furniture and walls.

How does Rochon manage to recreate such instant happiness with every new project? "I like taking up the challenge," he says. "My job is to combine the beautiful, the best, and the beneficial. And that's it. The trilogy of 'beautiful, durable, and useful' is based on the principles of a famous treatise by Vitruvius, a Roman military engineer in the first century. Whatever contemporary architects may say, this theory is still valid two thousand years later."

If the rule of the "three unities" is applied to interior design, beauty should come first, as the previous chapter illustrates. But what about the best and the beneficial? They represent the concept of luxury that Rochon defines as "the quality of an object and the way it is crafted." He adds that pride in work well done is one of the foundations of civilization. The work of the craftspeople hired by Rochon must obviously be beautiful, but it must also last—hence, be made of the best materials. The notion of temporary or disposable items is foreign to such artisans. Faithful to Rochon's design principles, these excellent craft experts in every field—marbleworkers, bronzesmiths, gilders, cabinetmakers, ironworkers, upholsterers, glassmakers, decorators, lacquer and ceramic artists—all supply him with the fruits of their handiwork and expertise. Nothing escapes Rochon's experienced eye; he oversees an interior down to the tiniest detail. He likes to design floorings, such as the one on the bar of the Hôtel George V in Paris; he won't let anyone else combine different marbles together or sketch the pattern of rug whose subtle hues must reflect the ambient harmony. He also knows that

PAGE 96
In the luxury of this Florentine decor, comfort is expressed through an abundance of velvet and brocade cushions and by the quilted silk bedspread.

FACING PAGE
In Geneva, reflected in the mirror on the door, an elegant old bureau adorned with hand-painted flourishes is the focal point in a softly decorated space.

the quality of the leather on an armchair, or of the silk used to line a wall, tells more about the refinement of a home than any words could do. When seeking advice on the choice of fabrics, he turns to his favorite colleague—his wife, Annick. To insure the harmony of every room, she collects samples of fabrics, wallpapers, and other materials in boxes. In each box, the juxtaposition of various textures in subtly different shades demonstrates a fertile imagination and a sure eye.

In respecting the identity of a given building, Rochon uses the key features and artworks that have made it famous. Thus the magnificent commodes and tapestries in the Hôtel George V are once again enhanced by a setting worthy of them. In order to underscore the difference between his interiors and that of a traditional hotel interior, Rochon will combine contemporary furniture with old furnishings and fixtures gleaned from antique dealers. Then he will artfully arrange them all, recreating the spirit of a private home within a hotel. Sometimes he will add personal creations, and here, his artist's talent is an additional asset, because he can draw armchairs, sofas, console tables, and lamps in a sober, naturally elegant way, with just a few strokes of a pencil.

Every personalized interior calls for works of art. Rochon loves to choose the paintings that will adorn the walls of a hotel. A valued colleague, Françoise Durst, is a framing specialist who brings Rochon's ideas to life by finding new settings for old engravings and making frames that suit the size and shape a given artwork—and given hotel. Sometimes Durst will commission talented young artists to paint frescoes and canvases in the spirit of the Old Masters. The actual hanging becomes a lesson in three-dimensional geometry, where the right height must be accompanied by the right lighting.

Lighting, in fact, is the grand finale that reveals the beauty of an interior. Rare are the specialists who know precisely how to light a space. "I know exactly what lighting I need to enhance a room or rare object," states Rochon. Once he has designed the luminous ambience he desires, Rochon will call on the skills of London lighting designer Sally Storey to install the lighting with utmost precision to produce a soft, intimate effect at any time of day or night.

Comfort is a question of body and mind, and it constantly evolves as revolutionary technologies affect functionality. Perhaps it is the bathroom—and, even more so, a spa—where the culmination of "the best" and "the beneficial" can be appreciated with greatest intensity and sensuality. Designed to delight the senses, these cutting-edge temples of well-being ritualistically wash away stress. Relaxing or getting back into shape in a heavenly environment is perhaps the true height of luxury.

FACING PAGE
Elegance and light
in a seventeenth-century style
permeate the entrance to the spa
at Florence.

ABOVE
Engravings in period-style
frames and chairs upholstered
in wonderful fabrics create
the sense of the hotel
as a fantasy family home.

A LEGENDARY HOTEL

When the Hôtel George V opened
in Paris in 1929, it served as a private
residence for an elite Anglo-American
clientele. Today, nearly a century later,
Pierre-Yves Rochon has employed
modern technology to create a warm
and luxurious atmosphere, thanks
to the confidence placed in him
by owner HRH Prince Al-Waleed Bin
Talal Bin Abdulaziz Al-Saud
and by Mr. Isadore Sharp, founder
and president of the Four Seasons
Hotels & Resorts group.
Realizing that foreign visitors
are highly attached to the eighteenth-
and nineteenth-century decoration
that epitomizes the height
of French style, Rochon incorporated
into his redesign the finest furnishings,
tapestries, and objets d'art from
the hotel's own heritage.

PRECEDING PAGES Entirely restructured, the Gallery overlooks an exquisite marble courtyard. Its dark furniture sets off the beauty of the colorful palette used here, including wonderful shades of yellow, straw, and beige that harmonize with the painted ceiling. The sumptuous Savonnerie carpet is impressive thanks to its visual impact and size—its 1,500 square feet of woven beauty require fifteen men to lift it. ABOVE Rochon designed the geometric pattern in the lobby by selecting five shades of marble. The new decor of the Gallery was designed around precious Flemish tapestries. FACING PAGE The Le Cinq restaurant enchants with its classic beauty, making it a pleasure to dine at its elegant tables with a view over the garden.

FACING PAGE AND ABOVE The bar evokes the library of an English gentleman, combining superb woodwork in cherry with beautiful parquet flooring. Guests come here to enjoy the hushed atmosphere of an English club by sinking into a velvet sofa or a Regency armchair beneath the bemused gaze of the gentleman in a hunting coat (an interpretation of a celebrated painting by Reynolds).

ABOVE AND FACING PAGE With an elegance worthy of the Petit Trianon at Versailles, the George V spa is an idyllic haven in the heart of Paris. Rochon devised a delightfully relaxing lounge, thanks to scenic wallpaper by the Zuber firm. Near the fireplace, Directoire-style furniture and objets d'art underscore the private, luxurious atmosphere of the hotel.

FACING PAGE How can the monotony of a long corridor be broken up? Here large circles on the floor serve as landmarks for finding your own massage room. Toile de Jouy paper lines the walls. ABOVE The spa's salon has a lavish Louis XVI decor that is just right for enjoying a cup of green tea between two beauty sessions.

ABOVE AND FACING PAGE A blue-and-white suite welcomes guests who appreciate the old French style. The Louis XV wall lamps, the sophisticated drape of the curtains, the gilded wood frames of the mirrors and paintings, the costly pedestal tables, and the harmony of fabrics and wall coverings all contribute to the elegance of the interior. As an iconoclastic designer, Rochon mixes styles and blithely combines a lacquered cabinet in the art deco style with a portrait of a noblewoman at the court of Versailles.

PRECEDING PAGES The bathroom exudes a luxury that matches the splendor of the suite. The pure gold on fixtures, lamps, and woodwork is set off perfectly by the marble and the palette of China blues. FACING PAGE The height of refinement is a shower that doubles as a Turkish bath. ABOVE The symmetry of the mirrors and twin sinks and the perfect geometry of the marble floor are softened by the collection of blue Chinese porcelain.

PRECEDING PAGES In the lounge of a suite where the windows are elegantly draped in silk, the comfort of technology can be found within a light and poetic eighteenth-century atmosphere—a perfect combination for guests. FACING PAGE The bluish framing of the engravings is in harmony with the striped walls and the design of the carpet in the entrance. ABOVE A geometry lesson in the bathroom: the horizontal lines are underlined by the gray marble and the light paneling. A crystal vase has been turned into a refined focal point. The curtains are held back with silk ties, and the stripes of the under-curtains—which add to the comfort of the suite—echo the wallpaper of the entrance.

II

PARADISE ON THE RIVIERA

At the tip of the Cap-Ferrat peninsula, overlooking the Mediterranean Sea, the hundred-year-old Grand-Hôtel du Cap-Ferrat has hosted all the great and famous of the last century, and it has just been thoroughly renovated. The hotel is set among palm trees and lush gardens, in the depths of a pine forest, and is a rare, wonderful gem of luxury and retreat. The regulars at this legendary establishment may never miss their summer poolside session at Club Dauphine, but now they can also discover the benefits of the newly created spa. This spectacular world dedicated to health and beauty treatments adds yet another dimension of comfort to this corner of heaven.

PRECEDING PAGES Rochon didn't hesitate to redo the Rotunda—originally built by Gustave Eiffel—so that hotel guests could enjoy the wonderful sight of the Mediterranean and the formal gardens. Rochon's careful harmony of beige and white yields a sublime lounge that generates a wonderful sense of well-being. Each detail was carefully considered—the floor is paved with beige marble and the *à la reine* armchairs, in the background, are upholstered in a subtle silk in harmony with the porcelain lamps. ABOVE Like the wall lamps in the Rotunda, the spectacular lantern chandelier made by the Tisserant Company for the hall enchants guests. It encloses rock-crystal doves that fly from branch to branch in the evening, lighting the wonderful molding on the ceiling. Made of nickel treated like old-style silver, the chandelier symbolizes, along with the cut-crystal Lalique table, all the poetic luxuriousness of this hotel. FACING PAGE From the Rotunda, between two large gilded mirrors and across the lounge, the entrance door with its fine wrought-iron work can be seen.

SALON
LES PINS

FACING PAGE AND ABOVE In the bar lit by large chandeliers of green Murano glass, the Directoire-style armchairs are upholstered in a soft green. In the dining room next door the sand-colored mosaic reflects the delicate pattern of the carpet in the bar. The bronze wall-lights and rock-crystal candles are mounted onto antiqued mirrors.

ABOVE The mural in the garden-level restaurant is a tribute to Jean Cocteau, who used to drop by from his nearby residence, the Villa Santo Sospir. It was painted by Michèle Letang, creator of numerous decorative frescoes. FACING PAGE From the columned terrace of one of the suites, the first rays of sunshine can be savored over breakfast.

PRECEDING PAGES Beneath a Picasso drawing soberly framed in black, the salon of one of the suites displays a silken hymn to beige and pale gold on the walls and in the silk upholstery. The poetic atmosphere is underscored by a lamp with a rock-crystal stand and a bowl in which yellow roses float. FACING PAGE AND ABOVE The soft harmony of gray and white contributes to the comfort of the bathroom. In the bedroom and lounge, a large sofa and a *duchesse brisée* are an invitation to relax. The silver wall-lights and doorknobs enhanced with gold are quiet witnesses to the fact that luxury can have a modern inflection.

ABOVE The spa is 7,500 square feet of heaven. A spiral ramp leads to this sybaritic retreat, where an artistic panel of tree roots symbolizes the marriage of nature and beauty. A statue of a Greek god greets seekers of beauty and health care. FACING PAGE Swimming counter-current in the glass-tiled pool is more pleasure than effort.

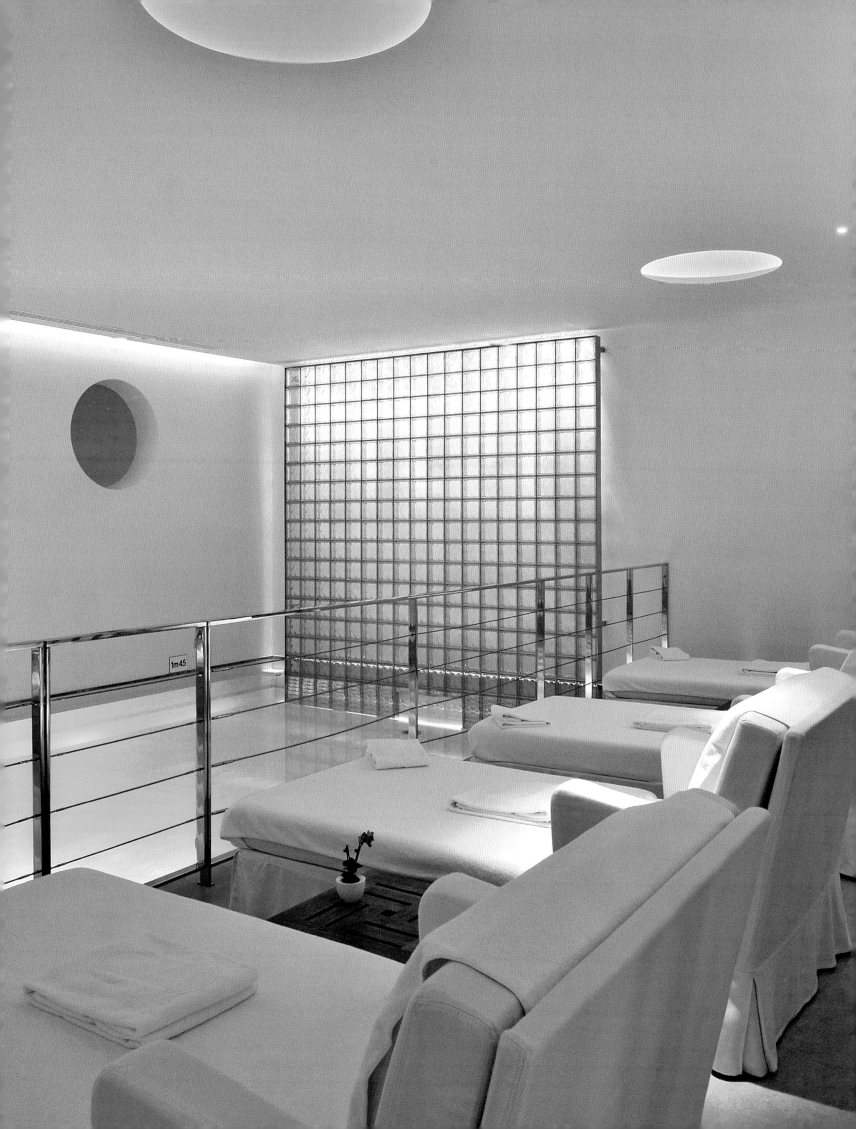

III

FRENCH COMFORT
IN CHICAGO

In the heart of the city, overlooking
Lake Michigan and the Magnificent Mile,
the Sofitel Chicago Water Tower flaunts
the bold, angular architecture
of Jean-Paul Viguier.
The interior decoration of this
glass-and-concrete tower was handed
over to Pierre-Yves Rochon, who
designed the spectacular black granite
lobby, the restaurants, bars, conference
rooms, and ballroom, not to mention
the rooms and suites where
a contemporary sense of luxury
is partnered with high-tech features
to achieve a sense of French
refinement and comfort.

PRECEDING PAGES In the lobby the floor is paved with black granite studded with light squares, and sofas with clean lines have been placed on carpets whose swaths of color evoke the work of Mark Rothko. ABOVE Respecting the exterior architectural concept, the striking colors of the interior bring some soul to an urban setting, from the hall to the dining room. Under the boldly designed clock, there is always time to make yourself comfortable and have a drink. FACING PAGE Several yards high, the daring mirrors of the large lounge multiply the geometric patterns of the interior design. In order to re-establish the equilibrium, the horizontal lines of the low furniture contrast with the vertical divides.

FACING PAGE "Time is money," says the large round rug in the middle of the Café des Architectes. The black leather armchairs by Philippe Starck, the tables, and an astonishing set of cylindrical light fixtures are all in keeping with the design. BELOW Seen from the outside, the name of the restaurant is written in the window in white letters against a red background.

ABOVE AND FACING PAGE The decor of this suite recalls the Bauhaus style. A large abstract painting (from the Galerie de Françoise Durst) structures the room around a square theme. The cushions on the sofa echo the padding of the famous chair by Mies van der Rohe. Objets d'art from around the world are in harmony with the modern decor, and all contribute to a sense of luxury and comfort.

IV

A PIED–À–TERRE
IN PARIS

Located in a quiet street just off the
Champs-Élysées, the Hôtel François I
seduces travelers with its classic decor.
Rochon cleverly created space,
despite the hotel's limited
dimensions. Contemporary details
and colors in sometimes bold
combinations give a unique style
to the suites, rooms, and salons
of this charming hotel. The warm
welcome and high level of comfort
make this an ideal rest stop
for travelers passing through.

PRECEDING PAGES Rochon displayed great ingenuity in restructuring and enlarging the spaces by employing a generous use of mirrors. The double doors of a wardrobe reflect an elegant suite where the dark tones of the Directoire furniture set off the golden silk fabrics. FACING PAGE Above a large black mahogany commode is a portrait of King François I of France, copied from a painting by Titian. The king for whom the hotel is named inspired Rochon to slip a touch of red into almost all the rooms, establishing a unifying thread to the interior. ABOVE In the lobby and hallway of the hotel, a mosaic of marble imitates Renaissance palaces in a geometric pattern of greens, reds, and black. Chinese vases in various shapes and colors evoke the distant lands that dazzled Marco Polo and other great travelers.

PRECEDING PAGES The mirror has been carefully placed so that the salon seems to look out on a charming winter garden—an attractive way to hide a blank wall and provide a green space in the heart of Paris. FACING PAGE The choice of flooring is of vital importance when designing an interior. Here, the marble creates a harmony of red in the reception area. ABOVE "It's really like being at home here," say guests. Objets d'art are tastefully set on period furniture in the lounge next to the reception area, and in other spots. A Chinese armchair, a steamer trunk, and period engravings contribute to a cosmopolitan, poetic atmosphere.

ABOVE AND FACING PAGE Nestling against silk or velvet, fair ladies who might have been painted by Fragonard or Boucher grace the cushions and curtains of this suite. Shades of yellow underscore the sensuality of the room, banishing the dreariness of Paris. Handsomely framed period engravings complete the setting, whose refinement extends into the bathroom.

FACING PAGE AND ABOVE The red, black, and gold come together in this suite in a contemporary reinterpretation of the Directoire style. The space is multiplied in the mirrors of the wardrobe; on the bed, vivid red and white create a vibrant contrast against the studded black leather bedstead.

V

A GEM FROM
THE BELLE ÉPOQUE

Overlooking the port of Monaco
where fabulous yachts are moored,
the Hôtel Hermitage is known for its
discreet charm. The hotel is listed
as a historic landmark, and renovation
of such a symbol of the principality
was a difficult task. Rochon injected
a new freshness through gentle
changes. As a counterpoint
to the indoor garden with its glass-
and-steel dome by Gustave Eiffel,
Rochon revamped the lobby to make
it more luminous, notably by adding
a mosaic in delicate colors.
The unpretentious yet refined luxury
of the rooms and suites makes
each one a haven of comfort.

PRECEDING PAGES Two steps from the Casino, the lobby of the Hôtel Hermitage is a promise of tranquility. The beautiful Corinthian columns, bathed in light from the windows, highlight the delicate pistachio green, and create several small, discreet lounges with comfortable seating in green and yellow, at each corner of the new mosaic. FACING PAGE AND ABOVE In this suite, composed of tones of beige and light woodwork, two brushed-steel doors open from the lounge into the bedroom. This architectural feature gives the lounge a very contemporary feel, while still remaining classic. The height of the ceiling seems to stretch ever upward and, depending on the time of day, the steel takes on the surrounding tones.

PRECEDING PAGES In the center of this salon, under the moldings of the rotunda, two beige leather sofas, poufs, and a low table in precious wood soberly structure the space that opens out onto a balcony with a view of the port of Monaco. ABOVE AND FACING PAGE Breaking away completely from the classic surrounding of the hotel, the Red Roses room captivates with its freshness. The curtains, armchairs, lampshades, cushions, and accessories all combine to create a feeling of a romantic reawakening.

FACING PAGE AND BELOW In these two rooms, contradictions are played with. On one side there are the regulated shapes and colors of the floors, walls, and bedsteads, in beiges and creams, and on the other side, textiles and objects in exuberant colors. The bedspread, cushions, curtains, and armchairs imitate the patterns of the Chinese porcelain. In the other room, the cream-colored backdrop is enlivened by shades of coral and red.

CHAPTER III

Exercises in Styles

> " I like mixing styles, adding touches of modernity to a classic image. I create unifying combinations. "

There are certain geographical places that can be said to have soul—because they were once the site of an historic event, perhaps, or the setting for a passionate romance. Time, however, can weary that soul.

Reviving the famous spirit of a place, making it once again unforgettable, is the tangible yet elusive goal sought by Pierre-Yves Rochon. Which is no easy task.

"When I accept a project, I steep myself in the history of the place—including the footnotes to that history—in order to create a solid foundation for recreating an idyllic reality," says Rochon. "I know immediately which architectural features must stay—such as the wonderful painted ceilings in the Four Seasons Hotel in Florence."

Work is then organized around these key features, which will be enhanced through the choice of volumes and colors. Next comes a thorough job of investigation, of rummaging through archives to find the right pictures, plans, and documents that shed light on the tastes and priorities of society at that time. Steeping oneself in the cultural context of the day, through works of art such as portraits and interior scenes, can provide a mine of valuable information about fabrics and furnishings. Once this detective work is over, the major lines of the design become clear, defining the overall theme of the interior.

"However, my work is certainly not about identical restoration!" insists Rochon. "Always keeping my overall idea in mind, I seek affinities and aesthetic connections between periods and styles. Just think of the fashion for *chinoiserie* in eighteenth-century interiors! I love that kind of juxtaposition. In my own interiors, a Louis XV *bergère*-style armchair can coexist with modern furnishings, a baroque chandelier of Murano crystal can cast light on furniture by Harry Bertoïa or Mies van der Rohe. But bringing a touch of modernity to an old building calls for a certain boldness and an undeniable skill. You have to follow a main thread, whether that is an architectural principle, a dominant color, or a pronounced contrast. You usually manage to get just the right balance by respecting lines, materials, and chromatic harmony. Sometimes I cultivate contradictions, I'll admit—for example I can stick a crazy-looking Far-Eastern-style bar into an art deco house! Nothing is more stimulating than reconciling

PAGE 168
Furniture designed
by Harry Bertoïa and
Eero Saarinen is right at home
in the bedroom of a historic
landmark house from the 1930s.
The blue carpet, chairs, cushions,
and blinds project the beauty
of a summer sky.

FACING PAGE
To enliven the entrance,
the black-and-white flooring
is criss-crossed by a lane of beige
marble. Subverting the symmetry,
the hall is framed on one side
by a console table and on
the other by a giant Chinese vase.

past with present, or exoticism with classicism, or giving visitors a knowing wink through an impertinent or jokey allusion."

Rochon's eclecticism, built on juxtapositions and the effect of surprise, creates a dynamic that rejuvenates the conventional, starchy atmosphere of grand hotels, without ever turning his interiors into museums.

He presents a theme, then complicates the picture with delightful anachronisms that draw visitors into his game—or rather, into his dream. On arriving at a hotel, guests become actors, finding themselves on stage. At the Hôtel des Bergues in Geneva, eternal lovers of Elizabeth of Austria—Sissi—can seek solace in a cup of tea in a blue sitting room. At Les Crayères in Reims, a gourmet aesthete can sit beneath the glass ceiling of a dining room or indoor garden—created from scratch. Decorative touches pay vibrant tribute to Chinese and Japanese culture even as they remain light and poetic. The Middle-Eastern tearoom in the Hôtel du Lac in Vevey plunges guests into the delightfully mysterious intimacy of a harem, under the pensive gaze of an odalisque. In Shanghai, thanks to art deco furnishing, Western influences provide balance to a sublime, sensual, stimulating world, where the refinement of Chinese civilization eerily echoes the strict geometry of the 1930s. Sometimes—as at the Hôtel Keppler in Paris, or in a private home by the sea—we discover the fundamental complementarity of black and white, a bracing two-note composition masterfully orchestrated by Rochon. Positive versus negative, plain versus textured: the play of radical oppositions includes fabrics, ceramics, and artworks, occasionally punctuated by a red cushion or the pink petals of an orchid.

By playing with extremes and creating unexpected connections, Rochon delights visitors with a new sense of splendor.

To convey a love of beauty is perhaps the most noble of callings.

FACING PAGE
Playing with blacks and grays is a stylistic exercise symbolizing elegance and refinement. In Florence, civilized comfort and refined technology are the essential elements of this spa. Beneath a large *grisaille* picture that evokes the enigmatic atmosphere of Piranesi's engravings, Directoire-style chairs match a delightful round table with mosaic top.

ABOVE
Bluish-gray interspersed with beige silks creates a tranquil atmosphere in this room in the Hôtel George V.

A VIEW
OVER LAKE GENEVA

"When I saw this hotel, I thought
of Empress Elizabeth of Austria,
who came to relax on these shores
with their view of the snow-capped
Alpine peaks. I was inspired by
the happy years that Sissi spent in
Geneva," says Pierre-Yves Rochon.
On the edge of the lake, the oldest
luxury hotel in Switzerland and
headquarters of diplomacy,
the Hôtel des Bergues combines
luxury, calm, and pleasure.
The hotel was entirely reconstructed.
Revisiting the hotel's glorious past,
Rochon did not hesitate
to mix styles and periods to restore
the decor to its former splendor.
Privileged travelers treasure
the light, opulent atmosphere created
by the colors, materials, and lighting
of the imposing rooms and suites.

PRECEDING PAGES How can an unappealing space, the area where guests wait for the lifts, be transformed into a beautiful lounge? Here, a cozy area where guests can pause before moving to another floor or another ambience has replaced a gloomy corner. A harmony of navy blue velvet is highlighted with huge eighteenth-century gilt-bronze wall lamps, while one of the Vatican's Swiss Guards stands at attention. ABOVE When flames crackle in the fireplace at tea time, guests can enjoy a relaxing moment on the large blue sofas, while admiring the authentic eighteenth-century Chinese portraits, hanging among landscapes and Western portraits. FACING PAGE Rochon chose a light, romantic atmosphere for the blue sitting room, enlivening the classic furniture with a touch of Orientalism. The toile de Jouy fabrics find a stimulating counterpoint in the blue Chinese porcelain, carrying on the theme of blue and white.

PRECEDING PAGES There is a mix of styles in this elegant dining room, where the English table is set for a family reunion. The imposing black marble fireplace is flanked by period panels featuring Italian figures. The crystal pendants of a Regency chandelier glitter against the ice-blue woodwork, itself set off by the gilding on frames and chairs. ABOVE A period teapot is testament to the refinement of this exclusive hotel. Even when the sky is gray, the silken draperies of the Royal Suite generate a warm, lavish atmosphere. Rediscovered during the hotel's renovation, the beautifully high ceilings add to the luxury and harmony of the room. FACING PAGE Placing a large claw-foot bathtub in front of the window and in the middle of the bathroom is an unusual practice, but one which brings a theatrical note to the ritual of bathing.

PRECEDING PAGES The magnificent volumes of this suite convey a thoroughly elegant contemporary spirit. The interior reflects a marvelous sense of balance, as the clean lines of the sideboard sustain the geometry of the space. The refined ambience of cool tones is accentuated by the choice of shimmering satin fabrics graced by silk-thread trimmings. ABOVE Beneath monochromatic abstract paintings, armchairs designed by Warren Platner in the 1960s surround a Directoire-style table of Italian origin whose black-lacquer top reflects the Murano chandelier. The bathroom, connected to the suite through a glass partition and a play of Venetian blinds, receives daylight. FACING PAGE Rising from floor to ceiling, dark gray padded leather paneling backs a Louis XV-style bedstead. The niches built into the exotic wood columns are an original way of replacing bedside tables in a narrow room.

II

AVENUE MONTAIGNE

Like a family home, the Hôtel San Régis
in Paris—superbly located
between the Champs-Élysées
and the Seine—seems to have existed
forever, welcoming travelers with friendly
warmth. For years it had been
highly appreciated by connoisseurs
for its elegance, but nevertheless this small
but exclusive hotel needed renovation.
The sharp sense of colors and proportions,
and the relationship between period
paintings and furniture belonging
to the heritage of the hotel, are exercises
in style executed with mastery
by Rochon.

PRECEDING PAGES Decorated with eighteenth-century paneling, the lounge of the hotel captivates guests with its hushed atmosphere. In front of blazing fires, lit once the weather turns cold, are velvet-upholstered armchairs, a Louis XV commode, and unusual bronze lamps with spiral bases, giving guests the impression of a private mansion where traditional habits and manners have survived. FACING PAGE The upper level of the lounge overlooks an indoor garden where hothouse palms and orchids provide an exotic note. ABOVE At the foot of the staircase the doors of the elevator are coordinated with the woodwork. A *Braquenié* pattern graces the walls of the small breakfast room and light paneling beautifully complements a seventeenth-century commode.

PRECEDING PAGES This attic room in red and blue is one of the most popular. Its personal feel, enhanced by refined details, creates a sense of well-being. The calico patterns on the walls are the perfect complement to the English mahogany furniture. FACING PAGE AND ABOVE All the rooms in the Hôtel San Régis have been fitted out with delightful period paintings and furniture. Although the rooms on the lower floor are larger, the rooms at the top are more popular due to their cozy charm and wonderful view of the Eiffel Tower and Grand Palais.

III

A HOUSE
BY THE SEA

Classed as a historical monument,
this house from the 1930s
represents an incredible example
of design. Pierre-Yves Rochon
restructured and renovated it from top
to bottom to restore its quality
and original charm, while conserving
the Moroccan element that existed
in certain rooms. He created
subtle relationships between works
of art and art deco furniture,
incorporating parts of his collections
to give life to this unique place.

PRECEDING PAGES Created from scratch, the winter garden goes around the façade. A round table echoes the curves of the bay and, depending on the weather, dinner may be served here against a backdrop of stunning sea views. ABOVE An Orientalist fresco by Michèle Letang presides over the blue waters of the pool, evoking the stylized landscapes of the 1930s. Tall white columns and palm trees orchestrate the space. The overspill from the pool flows over white pebbles that subtly mimic the mosaic. FACING PAGE Black and white strike up a wonderful dialogue on the terrace. A spectacular carpet, specially designed for this room, complements the black mosaic on the floor.

FACING PAGE The hallway beckons visitors to enter an enchanted world—a reinterpretation of the highly refined style of the 1930s. The black-and-white checkerboard pattern on the floor sets the tone, while a specially designed wrought-iron mirror, typical of the period, reflects the staircase. ABOVE Although Rochon retained this original architectural element of the staircase, he leavened it by lightening the wood. A wrought-iron chandelier sheds light on a tapestry by Fernand Léger. Contemporary architectural details in black and white structure the space. PAGE 200 An unusual touch for the door of an elevator—three sailors etched on opaque glass, based on a design by Michèle Letang, remind us that we are next to a harbor. PAGE 201 A hanging lamp designed especially for this space lights a white table leading to a kitchen with a black-studded, white-marble floor. PAGES 202–203 The spectacular kitchen opens onto the garden bathed in sunlight, welcoming family meals.

FACING PAGE Sliding doors of gnarled mahogany open to reveal the refined ambience of the dining room. ABOVE Broken up by a succession of tables, the continuation of the lounge and dining room seems to go on forever.

PRECEDING PAGES In a tribute to the original decor, the study of the master of the house encourages reverie and reflection. Lavish silks that harmonize with the painted ceiling, the woodwork, and enameled tilework send the visitor on an imaginary voyage to the Far East. ABOVE A long velvet window seat adorned with cushions in a range of colors nestles in the semi-circle of the window and provides the ideal place to watch the boats. A copper basin is flanked by period mosaic tiling, in harmony with the decor of the study. A woman completely veiled in white, dating from the 1930s, watches over the study. FACING PAGE Picking up the Orientalist theme of the green study, an intimate bar is dressed in red, creating a warm and cozy room perfect for sitting by the fireplace with its period mosaic tiling.

PRECEDING PAGES This entire bathroom was conceived in order to give the tub with lion-head feet the starring role; it reigns supreme below a 1930s light fixture. The interior shutters filter out harsh light and are echoed in the adjacent dressing-room cupboard doors. FACING PAGE In a rainbow setting, a young girl's bedroom exudes bright charm. ABOVE Flowers and stripes converse in bold chromatic counterpoint. The same sharp colors enliven the bathroom, for which the furniture was specifically designed.

ABOVE AND FACING PAGE Japanese decor for a bedroom where geometry predominates—the cushions pick up the grid pattern of the four-poster bed. In this bedroom, which hints at a contemporary style, the bed, sofa, rug, decorative items, and pictures harmonize in blue. FOLLOWING PAGES Furniture by the big names of the design world—lamps by Max Ingrand, chairs by Harry Bertoïa, and a table by Eero Saarinen—creates strong lines that work well with this second blue bedroom by the sea.

IN THE HEART
OF CHAMPAGNE COUNTRY

Pierre-Yves Rochon's
first commission was the transformation
of a small neoclassical château,
Château de Crayères, into a hotel
of rare elegance. Thirty years later,
Rochon was asked to redo
the decoration—to play with colors,
materials, and atmosphere without losing
the original spirit of the premises.
Today, guests are invited to revisit
the eighteenth century thanks to a setting
that conveys all the luxurious savoir faire
of the great French tradition.

PRECEDING PAGES The more frivolous side of the eighteenth century is displayed in the Princess Bedroom, decorated in costly silks, period furniture, and paintings gleaned from here and there. Mixing styles with a sense of fun, Rochon played on shades of green that range from pale celadon to bright emerald. The magnificent curtains and under-curtains make the bedroom all the more comfortable. FACING PAGE Occupying the *fin de siècle* glass rotunda is the dining room, where ruffled silk curtains soften the bright light and Louis XVI armchairs upholstered in light tobacco-brown leather attend the table, making this the perfect place for family parties. ABOVE Cabinetmakers and plasterers have made an exact reproduction of the delicate designs of the original walnut paneling. A Regency fireplace, Romantic paintings, a magnificent seventeenth-century tapestry in hues of green, Chinese porcelain vases, and a large crystal chandelier recreate the *Grand Siècle,* but with a modern touch.

PRECEDING PAGES In order to enjoy the vast grounds in all seasons, a glass conservatory abuts the old façade of dressed stone. This new space, lit by a chandelier unearthed in a flea market, showcases several nineteenth-century portraits, and was created for this purpose. The armchairs are covered with a red carnation-print fabric. FACING PAGE The bar welcomes guests at teatime and cocktail hour. Plaid carpeting and curtains, and elegant red leather armchairs recreate the luxurious decor of an English club. ABOVE Nestled in a rotunda, a red sofa complements the shape of the glass wall. The interior window boxes planted with white flowers allow the garden to enter the room. In the same way, in the winter garden or the more contemporary beer garden, nature is reflected in the decor.

PRECEDING PAGES The smallest recess in the corridor can become an Oriental salon. The red of the walls and carpet lends a mysterious note to a corridor that could otherwise be commonplace. ABOVE AND FACING PAGE The blue of the bedroom is played out in a sophisticated combination of fabrics and toile de Jouy patterns. Every accessory and item of furnishing, from the little bench to the lamps on the mahogany bedside tables, although modern, are reminiscent of a forgotten age.

FACING PAGE AND ABOVE Guests arriving at Les Crayères expect to find the charm of a French château, but with today's modern conveniences. All the classic features have been underscored, ceiling moldings, marble fireplaces, and Romantic portraits, while canopy beds have been dressed with curtains of linen, not silk, to lend a more contemporary feel.

FACING PAGE AND ABOVE Here, the patterned fabric has been used sparingly on the walls to prevent an excessive effect. In the bedroom as in the bathroom, the blinds, the curtains, the bed, and selected items from the days of Napoleon III are enough to create an atmosphere of the past.

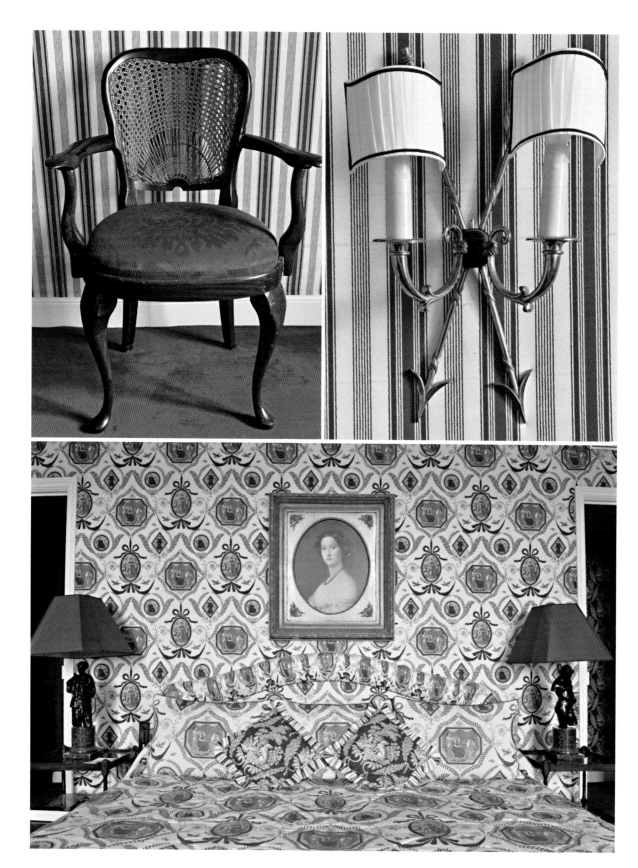

ABOVE AND FACING PAGE Stripes and toile de Jouy patterns play boldly opposite one another in the Red Bedroom. The large bed promises comfort and repose in front of a pink marble fireplace. The emblematic color of the lampshades, velvet armchairs, and carpet heightens the sensual ambience.

A CHARMING HOTEL
ON THE CHAMPS–ÉLYSÉES

Flaunting its ultra-chic,
exclusive side, the Hôtel Keppler appeals
to the discerning visitor in Paris.
It has just been renovated to bring
a contemporary interior into
a classic environment.
By playing on the opposition
of black and white, Rochon
has composed a veritable
two-note symphony that brings
out the true identity of the hotel, even
as he paid his usual attention
to the comfort and well-being of guests.

PRECEDING PAGES The intimate atmosphere of the Keppler's lounge invites guests to linger before retiring to their rooms. When temperatures drop outdoors, a fire crackles in this refined salon, reassuring new guests that they have indeed arrived safe and sound. ABOVE A play of stripes in positive and negative—one of Rochon's knowing winks. FACING PAGE A large painting can enliven an interior: a black-and-white interpretation of Sir Frederic Leighton's nineteenth-century painting *Nausicaa* greets guests at the hotel.

FACING PAGE It is hard to believe that this is a hotel reception area rather than a private sitting room. Lit by a crystal lamp, the concierge's black desk is flanked by white armchairs that welcome lucky travelers. ABOVE Two comfortable armchairs by the fireplace—the secret of classic decor. But here, it is the decorative details that give character: specially designed wall lights and mirrors, art deco sculptures, and vases in black and white.

PRECEDING PAGES Never one to shy away from bold colors, Rochon does not hesitate to use bright red in the bedroom. Filtered by the taffeta curtains, the light adds a sensual dimension and plays on the specially designed carpet. FACING PAGE Inspired by Matisse's drawings, the curtain and cushion patterns are decorated with black arabesques against a red background. ABOVE In this particular period hotel, the decor plays on black-and-white tones seen here in the fabric wall coverings, the curtains, and the carpets. As for the red, this continues into the bathroom.

ABOVE AND FACING PAGE A lemon-yellow armchair and cushions interrupt the dialogue between black and white. The black-leather bedstead projects its sober elegance in the modestly sized but extremely refined room. In the bathroom, the chromatic note continues on the walls and the shower floor.

This list of hotels is not exhaustive, but it includes establishments for which Rochon either designed and executed the interior, or undertook a complete renovation. In every one of these hotels, the rooms and suites, whether imposing or intimate, offer a warm, harmonious atmosphere—perfect for weary travelers seeking an exceptional experience.

In addition to the addresses given here, Rochon collaborated with chef Joël Robuchon to design the latter's famous L'Atelier restaurants, whose primarily black-and-red interiors can be found in London, New York, Taipei, Tokyo, Las Vegas, Hong Kong, and Singapore. Meanwhile, the Benoît brasseries in New York and Tokyo were designed by Rochon in conjunction with chef Alain Ducasse.

The page numbers below refer to photographs.

HOTELS

France and Monaco

FOUR SEASONS HÔTEL GEORGE V
31, avenue George V
75008 Paris
Tel: +33 (0)1 49 52 70 00
www.fourseasons.com/paris
see pp. 102–103
This hotel has regularly won acclaim for being the best hotel in the world since it was renovated by Pierre-Yves Rochon. The English-style bar with its blond wood and elegant armchairs is a popular meeting place. Just a few paces away, along a superb gallery decorated with precious tapestries, is the hotel's Michelin-starred restaurant, Le Cinq, where the cream of Paris society can be found.

HÔTEL FRANÇOIS I
7, rue Magellan
75008 Paris
Tel: +33 (0)1 47 23 44 04
www.the-paris-hotel.com
see pp. 146–147
A classic yet very intimate interior for a luxury establishment not far from Place de l'Étoile. The marble floors, period furniture, objets d'art, and skillfully lit paintings strongly appeal to travelers, who feel like they're in their own pied-à-terre in Paris.

HÔTEL KEPPLER
10, rue Keppler
75016 Paris
Tel: +33 (0)1 47 20 65 05
www.keppler.fr
see pp. 236–237

Behind the classical façade on a quiet street near the Champs-Élysées is a surprising interior in black and white, beginning with the lobby and lounges and extending into the bedrooms. Other colors also surface—the red ambience of suite 502 is a true delight.

HÔTEL RENAISSANCE PARIS VENDÔME
4, rue du Mont Thabor
75001 Paris
Tel: +33 (0)1 40 20 20 00
www.marriott.com/hotels/travel/parvd-renaissance-paris-vendome-hotel
A contemporary interior in a nineteenth-century building mere minutes away from the Place Vendôme.

HÔTEL RITZ
15, place Vendôme
75001 Paris
Tel: +33 (0)1 43 16 30 30
www.ritzparis.com
see pp. 80–81
The interior of this hotel, whose very name is synonymous with luxury, is the epitome of a kind of refined French style. Rochon has brought a certain Baudelairean "luxury, peace, and pleasure" to the establishment—ask for suite 417.

HÔTEL SAN RÉGIS
12, rue Jean Goujon
75008 Paris
Tel: +33 (0)1 45 61 05 48
www.hotel-sanregis.fr
see pp. 186–187
Perhaps the least known of the smaller grand hotels in Paris, this former private mansion was built in the nineteenth century. It is a favorite with musicians who perform at the nearby Théâtre des Champs-Élysées. The

intimate charm of its sitting rooms, its antique furniture, and its soft lighting, plus the soft hues of its ravishing bedrooms—each one different—create a delightful sense of well-being.

INTERCONTINENTAL HOTEL PARIS LE GRAND
2, rue Scribe
75009 Paris
Tel: +33 (0)1 40 07 32 32
http://www.ichotelsgroup.com/intercontinental/en/gb/locations/overview/parhb
This historic building was designed by Charles Garnier, the architect who built the Paris Opera. The hotel's spectacular ballroom, indoor garden, and Empire-style bedrooms are lavishly decorated. After having dined at the famous Café de la Paix (whose interior is a listed monument), spend a night in the magnificent red bedroom—you can enjoy the finest view of Garnier's Opera House from the bathtub in this royal suite.

SHANGRI-LA HOTEL
10, avenue d'Iéna
75016 Paris
Tel: +33 (0)1 80 27 19 35
www.shangri-la.com/fr/property/paris/shangrila
The Shangri-La hotel chain opened its first establishment in Europe in this historic private mansion, the former home of Prince Roland Bonaparte. Rochon was commissioned to design the interior, and has returned the building to its original grandeur while at the same time introducing contemporary and Asian touches, and all the modern comforts.

SOFITEL LE FAUBOURG
15, rue Boissy d'Anglas
75008 Paris
Tel: +33 (0)1 44 94 14 14
www.sofitel.com/fr/hotel-1295-sofitel-paris-le-faubourg
An elegant lobby with plush sofas and a 1930s-style bar. This very comfortable hotel has been created from two venerable buildings in a style that is both classic and contemporary.

DISNEYLAND HOTEL
Disneyland Resort Paris
77000 Chessy
Tel: +33 (0)1 64 74 40 00
http://hotels.disneylandparis.fr/hotels/disneyland-hotel/index.xhtml
This Victorian-style hotel is the most luxurious in Disneyland Paris. A favorite spot is the Café Fantasia designed by Rochon as a magical re-staging of the Disney universe.

LES CRAYÈRES
64, boulevard Henry Vasnier
51100 Reims
Tel: +33 (0)3 26 24 90 00
www.lescrayeres.com
see pp. 218–219
For travelers who wish to discover the architectural wonders of Reims and the secret cellars where great Champagne wines are created, there is only one address: Les Crayères. Even without booking a room you can enjoy tea in the indoor garden or organize a family luncheon in the skylit dining room overlooking the grounds—delightful opportunities to take advantage of the hotel's refined decor and setting. And don't miss the contemporary interior of the new brasserie, Le Jardin, in the grounds of the château.

HÔTEL LE ROYAL LYON
20, place Bellecour
69002 Lyon
Tel: +33 (0)4 78 37 57 31
www.lyonhotel-leroyal.com
On Lyon's famous square, Place
Bellecour, this venerable hotel was
entirely renovated by Rochon at the
request of the Institut Paul Bocuse.

HÔTEL DE TOIRAS
1, quai Job Foran
17410 Saint-Martin-de-Ré
Tel: +33 (0)5 46 35 40 32
www.hotel-de-toiras.com
Life in Saint-Martin-de-Ré centers
on its port, where this former private
mansion has been transformed into
a hotel. Rochon decorated it with
his usual sense of history, making
it a warm, elegant, and luxurious
rendezvous for locals for lunch,
as well as those who have come from
farther afield.

GRAND-HÔTEL
DU CAP-FERRAT
71, boulevard du Général de Gaulle
06230 Saint-Jean-Cap-Ferrat
Tel: +33 (0)4 93 76 50 50
www.grand-hotel-cap-ferrat.com
see pp.124–125
This legendary hotel sits at the tip
of Cap-Ferrat, like a great ocean liner.
Rochon used whites to frame the
views of the sea and its spectacular
grounds, whose powerful light changes
with every hour of the day. Guests
marvel at the orchestration of whites,
the large mirrors, the contemporary
furnishings in rooms and lounges,
and the chandeliers and candelabras.

HÔTEL HERMITAGE
Square Beaumarchais
98000 Monaco
Tel: +377 98 06 40 00
www.hotelhermitagemontecarlo.com
see pp.158–159
This traditional hotel in Monaco faces
the port. The elegant comfort of the
rooms is accompanied by the refined
decoration of the lounges where tea
can be enjoyed away from the crowds
thronging the casino.

MONTE-CARLO BAY
HOTEL & RESORT
40, avenue Princesse Grace
98000 Monaco
Tel: +377 98 06 02 00
www.montecarlobay.com
see pp.54–55
This contemporary hotel overlooks the
sea on one side, a garden on the other.

The suites with sea views are decorated
in Mediterranean tones. Pale marble
and blond wood add a fresh, cool note.
The spectacular dimensions of the
lounge are immediately apparent from
the entrance.

England

THE SAVOY
The Strand
London WC2R 0EU
Tel: +44 (0)20 7836 4343
www.fairmont.com/promo/savoy
This legendary hotel, with its
wonderful Victorian and art deco
interiors, needed considerable
refurbishment in order to recover its
original splendor. A new chapter
in the Savoy's history is now being
written by Rochon—the hotel offers
guests an ambience that combines a
highly Victorian floral style with art deco
features such as the black-and-gold
Beaufort bar and the Riverside
Restaurant overlooking the Thames.

SOFITEL LONDON ST. JAMES
6 Waterloo Place
London SW1Y 4AN
Tel: + 44 (0)20 7747 2200
www.sofitelstjames.com
The welcoming lobby of the Sofitel
London St. James, in a historic West
End building near some of London's
most famous gentlemen's clubs, has
become a favorite meeting place.
The warm yet elegant bedrooms
sport large Scottish plaids that recall
the building's history. The overall style
reflects a savvy blend of British and
French cultures.

FOUR SEASONS
HOTEL LONDON
Hamilton Place, Park Lane,
London W1J 7DR
Tel: +44 (0)20 7499 0888
www.fourseasons.com/london
The highly luxurious Four Seasons
Hotel overlooks Hyde Park.
Redesigned by Rochon, who
completely reconceived the hotel, its
interiors combine traditional English
styling with contemporary flourishes.
Particularly appreciated are the
mahogany-and-orange sitting rooms
and the wonderful idea of an "early
arrivals lounge" on the top floor,
where guests can enjoy a view
of the park and the comforts
of a private apartment while waiting
for their room to be ready.

Argentina

SOFITEL BUENOS AIRES
Arroyo 841
C1007AAB Buenos Aires
Tel: +54 11 41310000
www.sofitel.com/fr/hotel-3253-sofitel-
buenos-aires/index.shtml
In a quiet street removed from the din
of the city, this hotel, carved from two
nineteenth-century buildings and
a 1930s tower, combines French
elegance with traditional Argentinean
culture in its lavish yet welcoming
bedrooms and lounges.

Austria

HOTEL SACHER
Philharmonikerstrasse 4
1010 Vienna
Tel: +43 (0)1 51 456 0
www.sacher.com
see pp. 64–65
This legendary Viennese hotel is a
mandatory stop for opera lovers. Richly
endowed with a great collection of
original nineteenth-century paintings,
the Sacher's decor features a
magnificent play of colors in its rooms
and dark-paneled lounges. Guests feel
as though they are staying in a private
residence, and must make the difficult
choice between the green room with
its antique bed or the cooler,
contemporary blue-and-white room.

Bahrain

RITZ CARLTON HOTEL
PO Box 55577 Manama,
Tel: +973 1758 0000
www.ritzcarlton.com/en/Properties/
Bahrain
see pp. 24–25
On the edge of Manama Bay near
the tourist sights, this historically listed
building is among the ten most
beautiful hotels in the Middle East.
On entering the spectacular lobby
guests are awed by the tall column
of black marble. The elegance of the
rooms, suites, and lounges designed by
Rochon, not to mention the Turkish
bath, make the Ritz Carlton an address
worthy of discovery by travelers in
search of a something new.

China

THE PENINSULA
32 The Bund
Shanghai 200002
Tel: +86 21 2327 2888
www.peninsula.com/Shanghai
The Peninsula Shanghai opened in
Spring 2010 to coincide with the
Shanghai World's Fair, which made
the city the center of the world.
Rochon designed the interiors
of this glamorous hotel overlooking
the famous Bund in a subtle fusion
of Chinese tradition with an updated
version of art deco. Its grand lobby
with magnificent chandeliers and
its monumental tea lounge make
a lasting impression.

Egypt

SOFITEL CAIRO EL GEZIRAH
3 El Thawra Council St Zamalek
P.O. Box 732 El Orman Giza
11518 Cairo
Tel: +20 2 27373737
http://www.sofitel.com/gb/hotel-5307-
sofitel-cairo-el-gezirah/index
On the banks of the Nile away
from the noise of the big city, the
Sofitel Cairo El Gezirah has been
recently renovated. The cool, light
colors of the rooms contrast with
the lavish and eccentrically Eastern-
style decor of the Buddha Bar.
Space was not a constraint here,
so Rochon could give free rein
to his passion for devising lounges
with large windows that overlook
river and garden.

Italy

FOUR SEASONS HOTEL
FIRENZE
Borgo Pinti, 99
50121 Florence
Tel: +39 (055) 2626 1
www.fourseasons.com/florence
see pp.38–39
In the exclusive setting of a historically
listed Renaissance palazzo, Rochon
has staged his dramatic aesthetic
in an extremely refined setting:
the colors of the fabrics and walls
are coordinated with the pigments
of the frescoes on the ceiling.
Set in seventeen acres of grounds,
the Four Seasons Firenze also offers
the pleasures of spa and pool. A must.

PAGE 248 Samples of wool with evocative names and infinite shades are chosen for carpets and rugs custom-woven
to luxury standards, here from the Tai Ping company. FACING PAGE Extraordinary, decorative lacquer-work is executed today
in Anne Midavaine's workshop with the same dexterity displayed by the great Chinese masters.

Lebanon

FOUR SEASONS HOTEL BEIRUT

1418 Professor Wafic Sinno Avenue
Minet El Hosn
2020 4107 Beirut
Tel: +961 (1) 761000
www.fourseasons.com/beirut
A symbol of the rebirth of a city proud
of its traditional hospitality,
the Four Seasons Beirut has just
opened on the corniche overlooking
the harbor. Its classically elegant
sea-view rooms are decorated
with touches of local craftwork.

Netherlands

INTERCONTINENTAL HOTEL AMSTEL

Professor Tulpplein 1
Amsterdam 1018 GX
Tel: +31 20 6226060
www.amsterdam.intercontinental.com
This historic hotel is a favorite
with celebrities from around the world.
A complete makeover by Rochon
required two years of work. The
InterContinental's classically French
rooms boast views of the Amstel River.

Portugal

FOUR SEASONS HOTEL RITZ LISBON

Rua Rodrigo da Fonseca, 88
Lisbon 1099-039
Tel: +351 (21) 381 14 00
www.fourseasons.com/lisbon
One of the most elegant hotels
imaginable is perched on one
of Lisbon's seven hills overlooking
the valley. It is decorated in a blend
of classical and art deco styling.
Enormous bedrooms with lavish
furniture (such as the two-piece chaise
longue known as a *duchesse brisée,*
so rarely found in a hotel) and the
spectacular Almada Negreiros Lounge
with its black-and-green art deco
interior are special features of the
hotel's luxurious charm.

Switzerland

FOUR SEASONS HÔTEL DES BERGUES

33, quai des Bergues
1201 Geneva
Tel: +41 (22) 908 70 00
www.fourseasons.com/geneva
see pp.174–175
This legendary hotel is wonderfully
located on the edge of Lake Geneva,
within view of the city's famous
fountain. It is a veritable haven of
comfort, coziness, and peace. Suite 214,
with its contemporary color harmonies

of beige and brown is especially
popular. Passing visitors enjoy the bar
with its woodwork and pretty paintings,
a perfect spot for a light lunch or tea.
The hotel's elegant restaurant is the
place to go for a gourmet meal.

GRAND HÔTEL DU LAC

1, rue d'Italie
1800 Vevey
Tel: +41 (21) 925 0606
www.hoteldulac-vevey.ch
see pp.86–87
The rooms of this charming hotel
overlook Lake Geneva. Entirely
renovated by Rochon, who established
all the decorative themes of the rooms
and lounges, the Grand Hôtel du Lac
features a surprising Salon Oriental,
that is to say a tearoom straight out
of the Arabian Nights, bringing an
added touch of elegance and comfort
to a delightful setting.

HÔTEL BAUR AU LAC

Talstrasse 1
8001 Zurich
Tel: +41 44 220 5020
www.bauraulac.ch
If you don't have the time to stay
in Zurich, at least make a point of
having lunch in this hotel's Pavillon
Restaurant, very recently refurbished
by Rochon in an art deco spirit
favoring shades of gray and white,
set in the midst of garden greenery.

Syria

FOUR SEASONS HOTEL DAMASCUS

Shukri Al Quatli Street
P.O. Box 6311 Damascus
Tel: +963 (11) 339 1000
http://www.fourseasons.com/damascus/
Guests describe this fine hotel opposite
the museums of Damascus as
"paradise." Rooms and lounges feature
a blend of contemporary furnishings
with Syrian accents. The hotel's
three lounges have become the city's
favorite meeting places, while the lobby
is *the* place to be seen. To die for:
the Presidential Suite with its lavish
white-and-beige decor and its
surprising view of Damascus.

USA

SOFITEL CHICAGO WATER TOWER

20 East Chestnut St-Downtown
Chicago, IL 60611
Tel: +1 (312) 324 4000
www.sofitel.com/gb/hotel-2993-sofitel-chicago-water-tower
see pp.138–139
The hotel's spectacular architecture—

by Jean-Paul Viguier—is matched by
Rochon's interior design of bold
contemporary lines and colors.
The ensemble is a tribute to Chicago's
architectural beauty.

SOFITEL NEW YORK

45 West 44th Street
New York, NY 10036
Tel: +1 (212) 354 8844
www.sofitel.com/gb/hotel-2185-sofitel-new-york
Right near Times Square in the heart
of Manhattan, Rochon devised
an elegant and modern interior
to accompany the Sofitel's
contemporary architecture.

FOUR SEASONS HOTEL NEW YORK

57 East 57th Street
New York, NY 10222
Tel: +1 (212) 758 5700
www.fourseasons.com/newyorkfs
After having helped Joel Robuchon
to design L'Atelier restaurant in Paris,
Rochon collaborated with the chef
on other ventures around the world.
In New York, this entailed working
in the vast spaces created by famous
architect I.M. Pei. Says Rochon,
"I had to insert the concept
of L'Atelier in a true historic landmark
on the scale of a cathedral."
The trademark red-and-black theme
of the restaurant is skillfully set
in the beige-and-brown environment
of the Four Seasons' lounges.

SOFITEL WASHINGTON DC LAFAYETTE SQUARE

806 15th Street NW
Washington, DC 20005
Tel: +1 (202) 730 8800
http://www.sofitel.com/gb/hotel-3293-sofitel-washington-dc-lafayette-square
Not far from the White House,
this late nineteenth-century historic
landmark building now features
magnificent interiors in Rochon's
French-style art deco.

FOUR SEASONS HOTEL WASHINGTON

2800 Pennsylvania Avenue NW
Washington, DC 20007
Tel: +1 (202) 342 0444
www.fourseasons.com/washington
In the glamorous Georgetown
neighborhood, Rochon redesigned
the rooms and lobby of the east wing
of the hotel said to be the most
fashionable in Washington.
The contemporary styling of the rooms
is very Parisian in its elegance.

Ever since he founded his agency, Pierre-Yves Rochon has worked closely with a number of master craftsmen and artisans whose experience and skills contribute to the flawless execution of elements crucial to Rochon's interior design. It is hardly surprising that these artisans now receive countless orders from individual customers, as striking confirmation of their exceptional talents.

This selection is not exhaustive—Rochon appreciates the quality of work of other artisans and suppliers even if he has not had the opportunity to collaborate closely with all of them.

SUPPLIERS

Cabinetmakers and furniture restorers

COUNOT BLANDIN
BP N° 1–7, rue de Joinville
88350 Liffol-le-Grand, France
Tel: +33 (0)3 29 06 62 40
www.collectionpierre.com
This venerable firm is known for its copies of period furniture and its fine collection of modern furnishings.

PHILIPPE HUREL
Workshop:
16, rue de Chandelles
28210 Coulombs, France
Tel: +33 (0)2 37 51 40 38
Showroom:
4ter, rue du Bouloi
75001 Paris, France
www.philippe-hurel.com
An eclectic designer and producer of extremely high-quality contemporary furnishings.

LAVAL
20, rue de la Corvée Manette
88350 Liffol-le-Grand, France
Tel: +33 (0)3 29 06 63 31
Superb copies of period furniture.

LIGNE ROSET
23/25 Mortimer Street
London W1T 3JE, England
Tel: (+44) (0)20 7323 1248
www.ligne-roset-westend.co.uk
250 Park Avenue South
10003 New York, United States
Tel: (+ 1) (212) 375-1036
www. lignerosetny.com
See www.ligneroset.com for more store locations worldwide
Proving that there is no hard-and-fast distinction between decorating a hotel and a private home, Rochon often turns to Ligne Roset's great furniture designs for his hotel interiors.

POZZOLI
Workshop:
Viale Della Republica, 107
22060 Cabiate, Italy
Showroom:
Via Vittorio Veneto, 39
22060 Cabiate, Italy
Tel: +39 031 75 62 12
www.pozzoli.com
Famous for its extremely high-quality Italian furniture, this firm contributed to the renovation of the Four Seasons Hotel in Florence.

MICHELINE TAILLARDAT
Workshop:
Z.I. des Montées
21, rue de la Fonderie
45100 Orleans, France
Tel: +33 (0)2 38 51 24 03
Showroom:
44, avenue Marceau
75008 Paris, France
Tel: +33 (0)1 47 20 17 12
www.taillardat.fr
This company produces what are probably the finest copies of period furniture for the luxury suites and apartments designed by Rochon for exclusive hotels.

Framer

GALERIE FRANCOISE DURST
15, rue Tour
75116 Paris, France
Tel: +33 (0)1 45 24 73 00
For over thirty years, art framer Françoise Durst has been contributing to Rochon's interiors, where artworks are so crucial in creating an atmosphere. Her framing has certainly played a part in the designer's success and popularity.

Metalwork

LES MÉTALLIERS CHAMPENOIS
11, rue des Létis, Z.A.
51430 Bezannes, France
Tel: +33 (0)3 26 36 21 33
www.l-m-c.com
This workshop executes or restores the spectacular skylights and glass-and-metal structures in Rochon's designs, as seen for example at Les Crayères in Reims.

Lighting

ART ET FLORITUDE
Z.A. Les Ouches
Route de Santranges
45630 Beaulieu-sur-Loire, France
Tel: +33 (0)2 38 35 88 25
www.artetfloritude.fr
Using metal and porcelain, the designers draw inspiration from period pieces to produce contemporary lighting fixtures based around foliate motifs.

BAGUÈS LUMINAIRES
73, avenue Daumesnil
75012 Paris, France
Tel: +33 (0)1 43 41 53 53
www.bagues-france.com
Rochon particularly likes the crystal-bird wall lamps made by this famous firm, which he has used even in bathrooms—at the Paris Ritz, for example.

BRONZE D'ART FRANÇAIS
Parc Wilson, 31, rue Wilson
69150 Lyon-Décines, France
Tel: +33 (0)4 72 02 04 55
www.bronze-art-francais.fr
An extremely reputable firm in Lyon known for its top-quality bronze light fixtures.

The two companies listed below regularly work with Rochon, who appreciates their extraordinary range of light fixtures from the eighteenth, nineteenth, and twentieth centuries. They are responsible for the spectacular effects specially created for the lobbies of grand hotels such as the George V in Paris (Delisle) and the fabulous lantern in the Grand-Hôtel du Cap-Ferrat on the Riviera (Tisserant).

DELISLE
4, rue du Parc Royal
75003 Paris, France
Tel: +33 (0)1 42 72 21 34
www.delisle.fr

TISSERANT ART ET STYLE
9, rue Saint Sébastien
75011 Paris, France
Tel: +33 (0)1 47 00 37 37
www.tisserant.fr

TARGETTI POULSEN
16, rue des Marronniers
94240 L'Hay-les-Roses, France
Tel: +33 (0)1 45 12 23 23
www.targettipoulsen.com
Rochon has often worked with this maker of contemporary light fixtures.

VÉRONÈSE
184, boulevard Haussmann
75008 Paris, France
Tel: +33 (0)1 45 62 67 67
www.veronese-sa.com
For various interiors Rochon has used the use Murano-glass chandeliers made by this famous brand. Indeed, it is with Véronèse that he has designed and produced his own chandeliers, wall fixtures, and lamps.

LIGHTING DESIGN INTERNATIONAL CONSULTING
Sally Storey
3 Hammersmith Studios
55a Yeldham Road
London W6 8JF, England
Tel: +44 (0)20 8600 5777
www.lightingdesigninternational.com
Rochon immediately recognized the talent of London-based lighting designer Sally Storey, who now regularly works with him to create the lighting that is so important to every interior. She executes the effect he desires, specially devised for each room and modulated according to the time of day.

Marble

L'EUROPÉENNE DE MARBRE
88, rue de Rivoli
75004 Paris, France
Tel: +33 (0)1 47 03 42 62
www.edm-paris.com
This company has developed a perfect relationship with Rochon, who places great importance on the reflections and patterns produced by flooring. He appreciates the skill of the firm's craftsmen and the wide range of colors, as can be appreciated in the lobby of the Hôtel George V in Paris.

Wallpaper

The following two companies produce extremely refined wallpaper. Some hand-painted coverings are done on silk, such as the ones created by de Gournay for the Shanghai Peninsula and the dining room of the Hôtel des Bergues in Geneva. Meanwhile, Zuber made the *grisaille* paper decorating the walls of the spa in the Hôtel George V, among other papers.

DE GOURNAY
Little Chart
Penshurst, Kent TN11 8ER, England
Tel: + 44 (0)189 287 1510
Showroom:
112 Old Church Street
London SW3 6EP, England
Tel: + 44 (0)20 7352 9988
www.degournay.com

ZUBER
3, rue des Saints-Pères
75006 Paris, France
Tel: +33 (0)1 42 77 95 91
www.zuber.fr

Fabrics and upholstery

The two upholstery firms listed below specialize in wall coverings, curtains, sofas, and cushions in both period and contemporary styles. Rochon calls upon them for all his glamorous projects in which fabrics are a key element of the decor. Each stylistic period, for instance, calls for its own choice of fabrics and way of dressing windows.

ATAD
29, rue Victor Hugo
93500 Pantin, France
Tel: +33 (0)1 57 14 07 00
www.siege-traditionnel.com

ATELIERS CHARLES JOUFFRE
47, rue Alexis Perroncel
69100 Lyon-Villeurbanne, France
Tel: +33 (0)4 72 69 46 10
www.charles-jouffre.com

Rochon also works with the following firms: Brunschwig, Canovas, Colefax & Fowler, Créations Métaphores (Métaphores and Verel de Belval), Dedar, JAB, Lelievre, Prelle, Nobilis, Osborne & Little, Pierre Frey, Rubelli, Sahco, Veraseta, Watts, Zimmer + Rohde.

Passementerie

The decorative trimmings known as *passementerie* provide a final touch of refinement to curtains and cushions thanks to the quality of braiding, piping, fringes, and tie-backs, which must all be chosen with respect to a given style. Rochon regularly works with the three following suppliers:

DECLERCQ PASSEMENTERIE
15, rue Etienne Marcel
75001 Paris, France
Tel: +33 (0)1 44 76 90 70
www.declercqpassementiers.fr

HOULÈS
Workshop:
2, chemin de la Coudrette
77123 Noisy-sur-École, France
Tel : +33 (0)1 60 39 62 01
Showroom:
18, rue Saint Nicolas
75012 Paris, France
Tel: +33 (0)1 43 44 65 19
www.houles.com

LES PASSEMENTERIES DE L'ILE DE FRANCE
Workshop:
14, rue de Verdun, BP n°1
95270 Belloy-en-France, France
Tel: +33 (0)1 30 35 70 39
Showroom:
11, rue Trousseau
75011 Paris, France
Tel: +33 (0)1 48 05 44 33
www.pidf.fr

Carpets

The quality of the wool, the refinement of the colors, and the choice of pattern all contribute to the beauty of a carpet. Rochon very often designs carpets specially for a given interior, such as those for a seaside art deco house (made by Galerie Diurne) or his Eastern-influenced interiors (Tai Ping). Meanwhile, the spectacular Savonnerie-style rugs (covering 1,500 square feet) in the Grand Gallery of the Hôtel George V in Paris were done by the Madrid-based Fundaçion Real. Rochon appreciates the work of all six firms listed below, each in its own particular style.

BRAQUENIÉ
27, rue du Mail
75002 Paris, France
Tel: +33 (0)1 44 77 36 11
www.braquenie.fr

FUNDACION REAL FABRICA DE TAPICES
2, calle de Fuenterrabía
28014 Madrid, Spain
Tel: +34 91 434 05 50
www.realfabricadetapices.com

GALERIE DIURNE
45, rue Jacob
75006 Paris, France
Tel: +33 (0)1 42 60 94 11
www.diurne.com

SERGE LESAGE
68, rue Arthur Béarez
59152 Chéreng, France
Tel: +33 (0)3 20 48 73 44
www.sergelesage.com

TAI PING
860 Broadway
New York, NY 10003, United States
Tel: (+1) (212) 979 2233
See www.taipingcarpets.com for more showroom locations worldwide

TOULEMONDE BOCHART
Z.I. de Villemilan
7, impasse Branly
91321 Wissous, France
Tel: +33 (0)1 69 20 40 30
www.toulemondebochart.fr

Decorative painting

Decorative painting is no minor art. Before being authorized to work on any French interior listed as a historic landmark, an artist is required to undertake several years of training. Rochon calls upon the experience and skills of these true artists when executing various interior details, such as the imitation wood in the English bar in the Hôtel George V, the woodwork in the new Shangri-La Hotel in Paris (Atelier Mériguet-Carrère), and the columns in the spectacular lobby of the Hôtel des Bergues (Entreprise Trouvé).

ATELIER MÉRIGUET-CARRÈRE
84, rue de l'Abbé Groult
75015 Paris, France
Tel: +33 (0)1 56 56 79 15
www.ateliermeriguet.com

ENTREPRISE TROUVÉ
11, rue Jean-Jacques Rousseau
94200 Ivry-sur-Seine, France
Tel: +33 (0)1 58 68 56 00

Lacquer work

ATELIER MIDAVAINE
54, rue des Acacias
75017 Paris, France
Tel: +33 (0)1 43 80 68 94
www.ateliermidavaine.com
Rochon commissions the Midavaine workshop to execute copies of lacquer furnishings and objects made in China in the eighteenth and nineteenth centuries, as well as to decorate furniture and screens, and even create—in a 1930s spirit—TV consoles, cocktail cabinets, and other pieces of furniture that make perfect companions to the art deco style rooms and lounges.

Mirrors

Contemporary techniques for working glass have led to surprising designs that Rochon has featured in his interiors. These appear not only in bathrooms, but also as doors, such as the one of the elevator in the seaside house. He regularly works with the two firms below.

ATELIERS BERNARD PICTET
47, rue Oberkampf
75011 Paris, France
Tel: +33 (0)1 48 06 19 25
www.bernardpictet.com

GUILLAUME SAALBURG
Techniques Transparentes
99, rue Molière
94200 Ivry-sur-Seine, France
Tel: +33 (0)1 71 33 05 05

China

The china, glassware, and silverware bring a finishing touch to the decoration of every dining room. The china in particular plays a crucial role. The choice of colors and visual impact are part of the ambience specially created for hotel restaurants, as well as, of course, for all the Joël Robuchon restaurants throughout the world. Rochon works with, among others, the following makers of tableware: Bernardaud, Deshoulières, Haviland, and Raynaud.

FACING PAGE Pierre-Yves Rochon's famous project boxes, in which all the different elements of interior decoration are gathered (tiles, fabrics, trimmings, paneling), can serve as a model for all amateur decorators who are keen to check the composition and harmony of their interiors.

ACKNOWLEDGMENTS

My thanks to my wife, Annick,
who is always honest about my creations.
My thanks to the owners, event organizers,
and exhibition organizers who chose me, trusted me,
and allowed me to create within the rules of art.
My thanks to the architects, contracting authorities,
lighting engineers, landscape gardeners, and engineers,
who have enabled me to carry out so many projects all over the world.
My thanks to all those companies who, by their professionalism,
have allowed me to execute all my projects.
My thanks to all the workers, who, from one country to the next,
have always respected my work.
Thanks to the craftsmen: the cabinetmakers, bronze workers, glassblowers,
painters, decorators, tapestry-makers, lacquerers, and florists who provide the finishing touches
of quality to my projects with their talent.
My thanks to the art galleries and to the artists
who have allowed me to showcase their talents.
My thanks to all the collaborators who are part of my professional life,
my everlasting dissatisfaction, and my demands.
My thanks to a life that gives me the leisure to dream, the possibility to create,
and the time for the all projects that are still to come.
PIERRE-YVES ROCHON

My thanks to Pierre-Yves Rochon who trusted me. My thanks to Jean-Marie Heiderscheid who brought this book into being.
My thanks to Christian Sarramon, Dane MacDowell, and Isabelle Ducat who put their talents together to ensure the quality of this work.
My thanks to Kate Mascaro, Sophie Wise, and Tessa Anglin who published the English edition. My thanks to Valérie Vidal
and Élodie Conjat-Cuvelier who followed this project through to realization.
GISOU BAVOILLOT

CREDITS

© Pierre-Yves Rochon: p. 13, 14, 17, 19, 22, 25, 27, 29
Photo © Fabrice Rambert: p. 15, 24, 26, 138/139, 140, 141, 142, 143, 144, 145
Photo © Erwan Le Marchand: p. 166, 167
Photo © Richard Waite: p. 16, 180 below, 185
Photo © Barbara Kraft: p. 28, 32, 47
© M. Cananzi, R. Semprini, Tatlin: p. 60, 61
© Mela Ferrer: p. 93
© Millington-Drake Teddy: p. 124
© Succession Picasso 2010: p.133
© Jérôme Abel Seguin: p.136
© Hervé Quenolle: p.144, 145
© Gérard Redoulès: p182, 184
© Christiane Vielle: p184
© Ben Nicholson / Adagp, Paris 2010: p.246
© Victor Vasarely / Adagp, Paris 2010: p.247

Translated from the French by Deke Dusinberre
Design: Isabelle Ducat
Copyediting: Lindsay Porter
Typesetting: Claude-Olivier Four
Proofreading: Fui Lee Luk
Color Separation: IGS, France
Printed in Italy by Gruppo Éditoriale Zanardi

Simultaneously published in French as
Pierre-Yves Rochon, Architecte d'Intérieur: Les secrets du décor juste
© Flammarion, S.A., Paris, 2010
English-language edition
© Flammarion, S.A., Paris, 2010
All rights reserved.

No part of this publication may be reproduced
in any form or by any means, electronic,
photocopy, information retrieval system, or otherwise,
without written permission from
Flammarion, S.A.
87, quai Panhard et Levassor
75647 Paris Cedex 13

editions.flammarion.com
10 11 12 3 2 1
ISBN: 978-2-08-030149-9
Dépôt légal: 09/2010